Growing Orchids at Home

Revised Edition

THE BEGINNER'S GUIDE TO ORCHID CARE

Manos Kanellos & Peter White

Contents

"An orchid flower means what is says. It does not fall to pieces like a lily; there is no shedding of petals or dropping away from the peduncle; no self-decapitation, like that of a fuchsia; no collapsing and dissolving, like a spider-wort; – no, there is never any of this; the orchid-flower is neither superficial, nor fugitive, nor insincere...If we mistake not, orchid-flowers have a grand future before them."

James Brooke, 1872

The orchid family

Phalaenopsis

Orchids evolved between 76 and 105 million years ago, and they can be found in every corner of the world from tropical rainforests to the Scottish Highlands. There are over 26,000 species in the orchid family (Orchidaceae) and with over 110,000 registered hybrids created in orchid nurseries in the past 150 years, the entire orchid family is easily the largest plant family.

Orchids in the wild

Orchids native to cold countries (where there is frost in winter) such as Britain are terrestrial, which means they grow in soil.

Terrestrial orchids are also found in the tropics, but the majority of tropical orchids are

A typical orchid flower (Phalaenopsis)

A wild cascading Cymbidium *orchid (*C. aloifolium*)*

perennial epiphytes, which grow on trees or shrubs, or lithophytes, which grow on rocks. They are not parasites as they don't take any nutrients from the plant they are growing upon, they use it only for support.

Orchid growth

Orchids grow in two ways – upwards from a central point (known as monopodial growth) or laterally (known as sympodial growth).

Monopodial orchids, such as *Phalaenopsis*, *Vanda* and *Vanilla*, have fleshy leaves and produce a succession of new leaves from the top of the plant, growing taller accordingly, and flowering from the space between the leaf bases. The stem of an orchid that grows in this way can reach several metres high. What this means for *Phalaenopsis* and *Vanda* orchids grown at home is that if they are not repotted regularly they will develop a long stem that needs to be shortened in order to accommodate the orchid in a suitable pot (see page 31).

Sympodial orchids, such as cymbidiums, cambrias, cattleyas and dendrobiums, usually have a front (the newest growth) and a back (the oldest growth). The plant produces a series of adjacent shoots from rhizomes, which grow to a certain size, bloom, and then stop growing. The growth continues with the development of new shoots with their own leaves and roots, sprouting from, or next to, those of the previous year. While a new shoot is developing, the rhizome may start its growth again from an 'eye' (an undeveloped bud), thereby branching.

Sympodial orchids have visible pseudobulbs which store food and water and enable them to survive in harsh environments. The pseudobulbs can be many shapes – rounded, pear-shaped, tubular, flat, conical – with leaves on the top

Sympodial orchids grow laterally rather than vertically, following the surface of their support.

The bee orchid (Ophrys apifera) is remarkable as an example of sexually-deceptive pollination and floral mimicry.

and they may grow for years or wither after few growing seasons. The practical implication for this type of orchid grown at home is that they will develop into bigger plants over time, with more pseudobulbs and more flowering stems. The old pseudobulbs will need to be removed when they become yellow and wrinkly.

Orchid pollination

There are many different types of orchids – often with a very different appearance to the well-known orchids you can buy as houseplants – and their pollination mechanisms are the most complex in the plant world. The pollen is always in lumps of thousands of pollen grains, called pollinia, with a sticky patch which fixes on to the pollinator when it brushes past. Once stuck to the pollinator and transported to the next flower they are caught in the sticky cavity of the flower stigma and get pulled off – pollination has occurred.

Because their pollen does not get distributed in the air, orchids are ideal houseplants for hay fever sufferers.

Seeds and germination

The fertilised seeds take up to a year to mature and are minute, like dust, with up to three million seeds in a seed pod just 5 cm in size. Even tiny, native English orchids can have 20 or more seedpods with 80,000 seeds per pod. When they ripen, the seed pods split open and the seed is blown for miles by the wind. Orchid seeds have no food reserves, unlike the seeds of other plants such as beans or conkers, and can only germinate if they land on a piece of ground (or a tree or rock in the case of many tropical orchids) which has tiny fungal mycorrhizae living there. The fungi enter the seed and in so doing they provide the orchid with sugars and nutrients – its vast extensive network of fungal strands acts as an extensive root system for the seed. Once the seed has germinated and the plant has grown, a different fungus may take over to continue to provide food for the plant.

Pyramidal orchid (Anacamptis pyramidalis) growing wild in a meadow in the Cotswolds

A short history of orchid growing

Although the Chinese have been growing orchids in their gardens for over 2,000 years, the first recorded 'exotic' orchid in Europe arrived in England from the Bahamas in 1731. Orchid cultivation began when church missionaries, army personnel and explorers started sending plants back home to friends and patrons. In 1787, horticulturists at the Royal Botanic Gardens, Kew were the first to bring the tropical *Prosthechea cochleata*, the cockleshell orchid, into bloom in Britain, and by 1794, fifteen tropical orchids were grown successfully at Kew, almost all of them from the West Indies. As the interest in growing exotic plants took off, the nurseries of the 19th century dispatched plant-hunters far and wide in search of new species.

From the first part of the 19th century, those who could afford to have a heated glasshouse in their garden sought to fill it with these exotic and mysterious plants that thrived high up in the forest canopy without visible nourishment, in some of the most remote and beautiful regions on earth. Possessing orchids was a sign of social success and those who could afford it became enthusiasts – 'orchidelirium' (or 'orchidmania') was born and plant-hunters, scouring the world's wildest areas to gather exotic plants for botanical gardens and private collectors, focused more closely on orchids.

> The first orchid-growing society was founded in Manchester in April 1897.

Wealthy collectors affected by orchidelirium would fight over plants at auction when new shipments arrived from the Far East and the New World, paying the modern equivalent of thousands of pounds for a single plant. Stakes were high for orchid lovers: if they didn't win the auction, they had to wait for up to a decade for a specimen to grow large enough to divide and be available for resale. Orchidelirium came in two waves: the first, during the mid-1800s, was small compared to the second wave in the last decades of the 1800s. London was at the heart of the global trade and where orchidelirium was most intense, but it soon spread across to Europe and the United States.

The popularity of orchids meant nurseries could make a handsome profit by collecting large volumes of plants. They sent plant-hunters out in droves – in 1894 one nursery alone dispatched 20 collectors – and the result was that natural populations of sought-after species were greatly depleted. The then director of the Royal Botanic Gardens, Kew, Joseph Hooker, was so dismayed by the scale of collecting and the effect it had on habitats that he stopped funding orchid collectors. But, by then, interest in growing orchids had taken hold.

The great orchid collections of the early 20th century were wiped out in the First World War, through lack of coal and gardeners to tend them. While there was some recovery afterwards, the Second World War and the austerity that followed destroyed the remaining great collections and orchid nurseries. By 1975, few remained in the UK. America, Japan and continental Europe, especially the Netherlands, and later Taiwan, became the standard-bearers for growing orchids commercially.

With the advent of centrally heated homes and micropropagation, orchids gradually became popular houseplants and today *Phalaenopsis* is the most popular houseplant around the world. Orchidelirium might seem like something from the past but an obsession with unusual varieties of wild orchids still continues in China and Japan. In 2016, a Chinese *Cymbidium*, valued only for the colour of its leaves and nicknamed the 'Emperor orchid', sold at auction for $100,000.

Various orchids are grown around the world for use in herbal medicine, the perfume industry, and even as cattle fodder. The most important orchid in the food industry is Vanilla, *prized for the unique flavour of its seed pods.*

Prosthechea cochleata

Commercial orchid growing

There are millions of orchids sold in the UK by specialists, garden centres and supermarkets; the vast majority of them are either grown in, or come via, the Netherlands. *Phalaenopsis* orchids account for over 80 per cent of all the orchids being sold.

Commercially, these orchids begin their lives in a sterilised laboratory as microscopic pieces of plant tissue taken from the growing point (node) of a 'mother plant', selected for having the best qualities from a batch of seedlings. These bits of plant tissue are placed in Petri dishes containing a nutrient-rich agar jelly. Plant hormones in the agar allow the plant cells to grow and multiply, but prevent them from growing any leaves or roots. As clumps of cells are formed they are cut up into small pieces, allowed to continue growing, and are then cut into small pieces again until there are tens of thousands of small clumps. These are then moved into sterile flasks and grown on a different sort of nutrient-rich agar, and the clumps of cells then begin to develop roots and leaves. The resulting plantlets will be genetically identical to the mother plant from which the node was taken.

When the young plants have a leaf span of about 5 cm, they are ready to be taken out of the flasks and transplanted into small trays with growing medium, and put into a greenhouse. The temperature and humidity are kept high to stimulate leaf and root development. When the young plants reach the correct size, they are transplanted into pots. These are made out of clear plastic to allow light to reach the roots. The pots are filled with bark to ensure the pot drains well and the root system is aerated. At first, the pots are placed very close together to maximise space efficiency. When the leaves reach a certain length, a robot picks up the potted plants and re-spaces them at a lower density. This is to ensure the plants have enough light and space to continue to grow at the maximum rate.

When the plants are big enough they are moved into a cool greenhouse. The drop in temperature triggers a stress response in the plants, causing them to produce flower spikes.

After several weeks, the plants are moved into a slightly warmer area to encourage growth of the new flower spikes and flower buds, and as they grow the spikes are attached to a stake to keep them upright. After the flowers open the plants are packaged and sold.

Most orchids are sold through an auction in the Netherlands in a 'Dutch auction' that ensures the best quality plants receive the best prices. Following the sale, plants are transported via specialised trucks to outlets in Europe and beyond.

In commercial orchid growing, seedlings are raised from seed or meristems on sterile agar jelly with sugar and nutrients added, and no mycorrhizal fungus is required.

Buying orchids

Although most people buy orchids based on the colour and size of the flowers, or sometimes because of the perfume, if you want to keep the plant in good health and enjoy it for many years the most important consideration should be the environment you can give it in your home. The temperature and amount of light an orchid receives are critical for its long-term health.

Orchids can live for many years and flower year after year if they are given the right environment to flourish. It is not uncommon for orchids to live for a decade or longer in the home environment.

If you bear in mind the conditions in your house and where you want to keep the orchid before you buy it, you have done most of the work.

Where will you keep your orchid?

There is a variety of orchids to suit different indoor environments and you can, of course, change the position of the plant from time to time. For example, you can sit an orchid on a south-facing windowsill in the winter to maximise the light it receives, but move it to a west-facing windowsill in the summer to avoid direct sunlight damage.

Avoid changing the plant's position when it is developing its flower spikes so you don't get a lop-sided flower display.

Bathroom

Bathrooms are often thought to be good places for orchids because of the humidity, but this is not always true. Humidity is not constant: steam generated by showers is very hot, sudden and often extracted outside quickly. Bathroom windows tend to be small with frosted glass which can make the light conditions too low for an orchid to flower. Some orchids – such as *Masdevallia* and *Paphiopedilum* – will grow well in these conditions but others such as *Phalaenopsis* need brighter conditions.

Kitchen

Most orchids will do well in the average kitchen, which will generally have good humidity as they

	Orchid type
VERY EASY	Phalaenopsis
	Dendrobium phalaenopsis hyb
	Cambria
	Ludisia
EASY Just need to recognise their different phases	Cymbidium
	Cattleya
	Dendrobium nobile hybrids
MORE CHALLENGING	Paphiopedilum
	Masdevallia
	Zygopetalum
	Vanda

Why choose it?	Key to successful growing	Temperature and light
Very long-lasting flowers in a wide range of colours.	The easiest orchid to grow and ideal for beginners. Allow to dry between waterings.	18–24°C (64–75°F) Versatile, will do better in a bright position.
Very easy to grow and distinctive flowers.	Similar requirements to *Phalaenopsis*.	16–24°C (61–75°F) Versatile, needs a bright position especially in the winter.
Distinctive, often fragrant flowers.	Keep them in a cool position, especially when not in flower.	10–24°C (50–75°F) East- or west-facing windowsills most of the year and south-facing in the winter (except *Miltonia*).
Beautifully veined foliage.	Light. Too much will scorch the leaves, too little will make the plant 'leggy'.	16–21°C (61–70°F) North-facing windowsill or inside a bright room.
Magnificent large flowers that last for three to four months.	Hard to kill. They need to be kept outdoors in the summer. Heavy feeders.	10–30°C (50–85°F) Requires plenty of indirect sunlight throughout the year.
Striking, exotic flowers.	Cattleyas have a rest period during winter when they benefit from cooler and drier conditions.	16–24°C (61–75°F) East- or west-facing windowsills throughout the year.
A distinctive flower display alongside tall canes.	Has distinct rest and growing phases, requiring different conditions.	13–20°C (55–68°F) Requires plenty of indirect sunlight throughout the year.
Alien-looking, unique flowers.	Requires good humidity and a moist but not wet growing medium. It can do well in relatively low light.	16–21°C (61–70°F) North-facing windowsill or inside a bright room.
Very distinctive flowers, compact plant.	Requires high humidity and a moist but not wet growing medium. It can do well in relatively low light.	10–20°C (50–64°F) North-facing windowsill or inside a bright room.
Beautifully coloured, perfumed flowers.	Can be difficult to reflower but they have very special flowers.	12–21°C (54–70°F) East- or west-facing windowsills.
Unique, large flowers in beautiful colours.	Requires a warm and very bright environment for regular flowering. Easier to grow potted in bark.	18–25°C (64–77°F) South-facing windowsill in winter, east- or west-facing windowsill during the summer.

A note about orchid roots

Orchid roots are different to those of other houseplants as they have to absorb water and nutrients from the air, literally. In the wild, a high percentage of an orchid's roots wrap around a tree for support and the rest hang down. It is this characteristic that means they need some special care.

The roots of most orchids are covered in a spongy layer, called velamen, which helps them to take up moisture and nutrients from the atmosphere. The green (or sometimes reddish brown) tip at the end of a root is the part which is actively growing and it is not covered in velamen. Inside the velamen there are spongy layers of water-absorbing cells; in order to withstand the dry spells they encounter, the roots act as short-term water storage organs. When the velamen is dry the root appears silver-white – this reflects light and in turn helps keep the roots cool. When it's wet, the velamen becomes transparent, you can see the inner layer of chlorophyll and the roots appear green. This is particularly obvious in *Phalaenopsis*.

Fortunately, orchids and their roots are naturally quite tough and they will withstand somewhat erratic care, which is one of the reasons modern *Phalaenopsis* hybrids are very successful as houseplants. Modern hybrids are also bred specifically to thrive in the average conditions of a modern home.

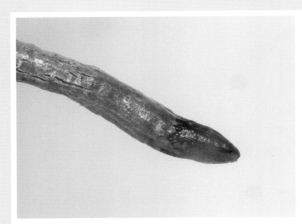

A growing (left) and a non-growing (right) Phalaenopsis *root tip.*

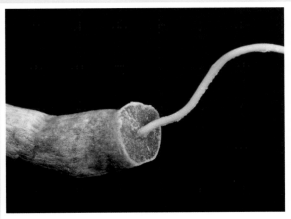

Cross section of a Phalaenopsis *root with velamen surrounding the root thread.*

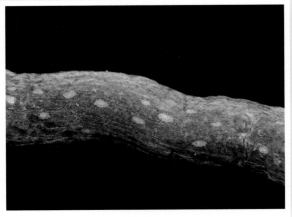

The white marks on the root are the stomata of the spongy layer – tiny holes through which the root 'breathes'. Air is as important to orchids as water.

don't tend to have many radiators, and cooking generates a lot of steam. Many kitchens also have large windows letting in plenty of light so orchids do not always have to be on the windowsill.

Spare room

Rooms that tend to be cooler and not always heated, such as spare bedrooms, could be ideal for cool-growing orchids. The only danger is that you may forget about the plant and not water it regularly. Cambria-type orchids or *Cymbidium* are suited to an unheated well-lit spare room.

Hallway and landing

If unheated they could be great for cool-growing orchids; if heated they are good for most orchids.

Bedroom

As orchids release oxygen at night – in contrast to most other plants – they are ideal for bedrooms. Bedrooms tend to be cooler than most other rooms so they could be good places for cool-growing orchids such as cambrias.

Conservatory

Conservatories, again, vary greatly in terms of conditions. A south-facing conservatory would be a very different environment to a north-facing one. Unheated conservatories would be too cold in the winter and too warm in the summer unless they are well shaded. A heated and shaded conservatory would be ideal in the winter for all cool-growing orchids, such as cambrias, *Dendrobium nobile* and *Cymbidium*, and for warm-growing orchids such as *Vanda*, *Phalaenopsis* and *Dendrobium phalaenopsis* in the summer.

Offices

As offices tend not to be heated at night, they are ideal for cool-growing orchids such as Cambria and *Dendrobium nobile* (but not cymbidiums which need to go outside).

Price

The price you pay for orchids depends on the pot size and the number of flowering stems it has. The price will be higher for a larger plant with more and taller flower stems.

Prices of commonly sold orchids also vary

The price of an orchid does not depend on whether the flowering stems are branching or not, so choosing a branching variety will give you a fuller display at no extra cost.

depending on the type – *Cymbidium* are the most expensive and *Phalaenopsis* are among the cheapest. This is because *Phalaenopsis* and most of the other common orchids are normally 14–18-month-old plants, whereas *Cymbidium* are older and are grown for about 4–5 years before they are sold.

Unusual colours and new varieties also command higher prices.

As with all things in life, you get what you pay for. Within the trade, orchids are normally sold at auction ensuring that the best plants attract the higher prices. The one time you might find a genuine bargain is the weekend after Mother's Day!

A good plant to buy: a Cymbidium *orchid with three flowering stems, plenty of healthy green leaves and a vigorous root system. However, this plant will need potting on after it finishes flowering as it is already pushing itself up in the pot (see pages 38–39).*

Buying tips

When buying an orchid, you need to check its roots, leaves and pseudobulbs, as well as the flower buds. If the plant is in a plastic sleeve, carefully lift it out of the sleeve (or ask the seller to do it for you) and inspect the plant. A good plant to buy will have plenty of green healthy leaves, many buds and vigorous roots.

Roots

Check the number and colour of the roots. This is easy to do for *Phalaenopsis*, which are normally sold in clear pots, but it can be a bit more difficult for other orchids. Basically, the more roots the better.

Phalaenopsis roots should be green or silver and not shrivelled. The roots of Cambria-type orchids should be a healthy, vibrant white, and make sure there is no green algae growing on

Avoid plants with yellow or missing buds. Yellow or reddish buds will soon drop. Orchids are slow-reacting plants and these buds will be the result of stress (too dry, too cold or too dark) that the plant experienced two to three weeks beforehand.

the pot. You can get a feeling about the roots of *Cymbidium* by squeezing the pot – it should feel hard and full of roots, but the roots should not be growing above the rim of the pot (a sign that the plant will be needing repotting soon).

Check the level of moisture in the growing medium; it should be neither very dry nor soggy.

Leaves and pseudobulbs

On a *Phalaenopsis*, look for a plant with three to four pairs of leaves. They should be firm and have a good, bright green colour, with no marks. If the leaves are blotchy with different shades of green this means that the plant has been standing in uneven light, causing chlorophyll to develop unevenly. Avoid plants with floppy leaves, which indicate possible root problems. Check for any pest or diseases.

For orchids that have pseudobulbs (such as cambrias), these should be green, turgid and healthy-looking. The more pseudobulbs an orchid has, the older and stronger the plant is.

Flower buds

An orchid should have about half of its buds open. It is even better if the flowering stem has branches, so the flowering display will be fuller. The buds are the most sensitive part of the orchid, so avoid orchids with yellow or reddish buds.

Paphiopedilum (slipper orchids) normally have one flower, so it is best to buy a plant where the flower has just opened.

A good plant to buy (Cambria 'Nelly Isler'): healthy green leaves, a good number of buds, two flowering stems and the flowers are perfumed.

An
introduction
to orchid care

As with all houseplants, there are a few factors to consider in order to grow orchids successfully. If you choose your orchid according to the temperature and light conditions your home can provide, you are already halfway to growing orchids successfully.

Temperature

Different species have different temperature requirements and can be broadly placed in two categories – warm-growing and cool-growing orchids – but you should be able to find a suitable microenvironment for both types. The average centrally heated house provides exactly the right temperature range suitable for orchids.

Most plants, including most orchids, need a period of lower temperatures to 'understand' seasons, as in their natural environment there is some temperature fluctuation between seasons. This requirement for lower-than-usual temperatures is very small in *Phalaenopsis*, and can normally be met in an average home, but it is more profound in the Cambria-type orchids and even higher for *Dendrobium nobile* and *Cymbidium* orchids, so it is essential you expose them to

When you buy an orchid, it is important to minimise any shock to the plant which can occur from a change in environment. An orchid would not cope well if you left it in a very cold or hot car for many hours, for example. Take it home and place it in a suitable position for the type of orchid it is (see page 10) and try not to move it again while it is in flower.

lower temperatures at the appropriate time. See pages 23–48 for more information.

Light

Orchids also have different light requirements depending on the species but most like bright conditions, especially in the winter, so it's a good idea to sit them on windowsills. No orchid likes much direct sunlight in the spring and summer, however, so as the sun gets stronger in spring you need to place some shading in front of the windowsill, or move it inside the room where it will not receive any direct sunlight. Of course, the sunlight an orchid

If the leaves become hot to the touch in sunlight, the plant is receiving too much light.

Orchid type	Temperature range	
Vanda	18–25°C (64–77°F)	Warm temperatures will help flowering.
Phalaenopsis	18–24°C (64–75°F)	Dislikes large temperature fluctuations.
Dendrobium phalaenopsis	16–24°C (61–75°F)	Cool temperatures during winter will be beneficial with the kingianum types.
Cattleya	16–24°C (61–75°F)	Can tolerate lower temperatures during its rest in winter.
Ludisia	16–21°C (61–70°F)	High temperatures will make the plant 'leggy'.
Paphiopedilum	16–21°C (61–70°F)	Dislikes large temperature fluctuations.
Zygopetalum	12–21°C (54–70°F)	Temperature fluctuations will help with flowering.
Cymbidium	10–30°C (50–85°F)	Needs to be moved outside during frost-free months.
Cambria	10–24°C (50–75°F)	Cool temperatures will help with flowering.
Dendrobium nobile	13–20°C (55–68°F)	Requires cool temperatures during its rest period but warm temperatures during its growing phase.
Masdevallia	10–20°C (50–64°F)	High temperatures will not help with flowering.

Orchids in general dislike draughts and large temperature fluctuations (Zygopetalum is a notable exception). They will all benefit from cooler temperatures when not in flower (the degree depends on species). Those with a distinct rest period (Cattleya and Dendrobium nobile) require different conditions during their growing and rest periods.

The start of sunlight damage on Phalaenopsis. *Characteristically, the part of the leaf shaded by the leaf above it is not affected by the sunlight.*

*Direct sunlight damage on the leaf of a Cambria-type orchid (*Brassia*).*

receives on a windowsill will depend on whether there are any curtains, blinds or any plants growing outside filtering the light that reaches into the house. Depending on the orientation of the house the light on one part of a windowsill can be significantly different to another part of the same windowsill. Exercise good judgement, observe the plant and keep an eye out for any signs of too much or too little light.

Orchid type	Placement for light
Cymbidium	Requires plenty of indirect sunlight throughout the year.
Vanda	South-facing windowsill in winter, east- or west-facing windowsill during the summer.
Dendrobium phalaenopsis	Versatile. Needs a bright position, especially in winter.
Cambrias (except Miltonia)	East- or west-facing windowsills most of the year and south-facing in winter.
Dendrobium nobile	Requires plenty of indirect sunlight throughout the year.
Cattleya	East- or west-facing windowsills throughout the year.
Phalaenopsis	Versatile. Will do better in a bright position, especially in winter.
Zygopetalum	East- or west-facing windowsills.
Miltonia	North-facing windowsill or inside a bright room throughout the year.
Paphiopedilum	
Masdevallia	
Ludisia	

Bright conditions help with flowering, in general, but no orchid likes much direct sunlight in spring and summer.

Watering

Watering is an essential part of orchid care – they should be watered as required but not too often. Overwatering (which refers to the frequency of watering rather than the amount of water each time) is one of the most common ways that people kill their orchids (and houseplants in general).

When to water – root colour, weight

In a typical house, orchids tend to need watering once every one to three weeks depending on the season and on how bright and warm their position is.

For most orchids, you need to allow the growing medium to dry out between waterings but the degree of drying out differs between species (see pages 23–48). In general, the best way to check whether an orchid needs watering is by feeling the weight of the pot and, in some cases, looking at the state of the roots and pseudobulbs.

If *Phalaenopsis* roots are green, the plant does not need any water. When the roots are silver check the weight of the pot. If it feels light you can water it. If not, leave it for few days. If the roots of a *Phalaenopsis* or the pseudobulbs (of an orchid that has them) are shrivelled, you have left it too long.

Using this method a few times will lead to a rhythm. If you follow the root, colour and weight method you will find that you water more in spring and summer and less in the winter, which corresponds well with the needs of most houseplants.

If you are in doubt about whether to water your orchid or not, don't. Leave it and check a few days later. You can correct under-watering but you cannot easily or quickly correct overwatering.

How to water

The simplest and best way is to water from the top. This way old salts, fertiliser or calcium from hard water are easily flushed out. Lift the orchid out of any decorative pot or saucer, pour plenty of tepid water through the roots in the inner pot and let it drain before placing it back into its decorative pot. You should aim to give the plant at least as much water as the volume of the pot and until you see good run off. Most orchids are sold in 12 cm pots so about 1 litre (2 pints) of water would be about right.

If you prefer, you can dunk the orchid roots in tepid water. Remove the orchid from any decorative pot and sit it in a bowl of water almost up to the rim of the inner pot and leave it to soak until the bark is thoroughly wet. You will probably need to hold the pot in the water with both hands to make sure it does not float, then weigh it down with large pebbles or similar. Soak for five to ten minutes, then lift it out and let it drain well before you put it back in its decorative pot.

One drawback of the dunking method is that the bark on the top of the pot can float off and expose the roots – holding the pot down with both hands should prevent this, as would covering the bark with stones. Be aware, though, that if you forget it and leave the pot sitting in water for a few hours, you will damage the roots.

Healthy silver Phalaenopsis *roots ready for watering. The few dead (brown) roots indicate that the plant has been overwatered some time ago but there are still plenty of healthy roots.*

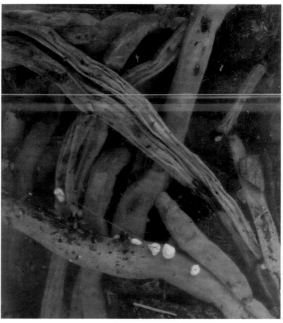

The high proportion of dead (brown) roots indicates overwatering. There are a few healthy green roots, so the plant should be able to recover if the frequency of watering is adjusted.

of the pot if possible, but make sure you weigh the pot down with something heavy) for 20–30 minutes and then let it drain.

If the leaves have become dehydrated and floppy because the plant has no roots (probably due to overwatering) it should obviously not be dunked. You can instead put the plant into a transparent polythene bag to keep the humidity high until you see signs of new roots, but there is no guarantee this will work.

Water type

Water quality is also an essential factor in maintaining healthy roots. Most orchids can tolerate hard water with few side effects on their roots for long periods, but if you live in a hard-water area it is a good idea to periodically water your orchids with soft water or rainwater to flush through any salts that have built up.

Orchids – like all houseplants – are best watered with tepid water to avoid any temperature shocks. Tepid water also re-hydrates roots better and faster, whereas cold water cools the roots and restricts their growth. You can use tepid boiled water or water from filter jugs, but do not use water from domestic water softeners as these use salts to soften the water.

Orchids potted in coir (coco) should not be dunked in water.

Dunking is particularly useful if you have left your plant without watering for so long that the leaves have become dehydrated and floppy. Dunk the orchid in tepid water (up to the rim

Wrinkled leaves on a Vanda *due to underwatering*

Floppy Phalaenopsis *leaves due to underwatering*

Humidity

Like all houseplants of tropical origin, orchids thrive in a humid environment. In their native tropical forests (and the nurseries where orchids are grown) the humidity is 70–90 per cent, but central heating makes the home environment very dry, especially in winter. When the heating has been on for most of the day the humidity can be around 30–40 per cent.

A simple way to increase humidity around your orchids is to spray them regularly, say two to three times per week. The best time of day to spray is in the morning. Take care not to leave any water sitting in the core of the plant right where the top two leaves meet. Spray the leaves (apart from some types such as *Paphiopedilum*, *Zygopetalum* and *Ludisia*), the aerial roots, and the top of the growing medium.

Spray orchids with soft water or rainwater, but avoid hard water as it will leave white marks on the leaves. Alternatively, spray them with a foliar feed. There are many available on the market specifically for orchids, or you could make your own: dilute a good-quality orchid-specific fertiliser at half the strength recommended for watering.

Orchids will not thrive in low-humidity environments. Their leaves will tend to be smaller, twisted and more brittle, and in cases of very low humidity the leaves will start splitting.

Another good way to increase humidity is to sit your orchids on a humidity tray. It can be used in combination with spraying or on its own. Sit your orchids on top making sure the bottoms of the pots do not touch the water – the water will increase the humidity around the plants as it evaporates. Keep an eye on the water level and top up as necessary.

You can buy purpose-made humidity trays or use a saucer or deep tray. Fill the tray or saucer with a non-organic material like gravel, grit or hydroleca, and then fill with water almost to the top.

A humidity tray positioned out of direct sunlight is a good way to look after your orchids, especially if you go away on holiday. Give the plants a good watering before you go, sit them on a humidity tray away from direct sunlight and go on holiday for two to three weeks with peace of mind.

Feeding

Orchids need regular feeding and it is important to use a urea-free fertiliser specifically formulated for orchids. These are weaker than regular houseplant fertilisers, which are likely to damage the exposed roots and lead to root burn.

Not every product sold as 'orchid fertiliser' is necessarily great for orchids. Use an orchid-specific fertiliser that contains all the essential nutrients that plants need for vigorous, healthy growth and prolonged flowering. This is especially important for orchids, which are normally grown in bark or an inert material that does not contain any nutrients. So look on the label – the more nutrients a fertiliser contains the better.

Make sure the fertiliser does *not* contain urea (or ureic nitrogen). Urea is a cheap form of synthetic nitrogen which cannot be taken up by plants. It needs to be broken down by soil bacteria which are not present in bark, so it accumulates around the orchid roots and damages them.

The best orchid fertilisers contain humic acid – an organic substance that makes nutrients more available to plants.

Most orchid fertilisers come in two types: a 'Grow' (or 'Spring/Summer') formulation which is high in nitrogen and a 'Bloom' (or 'Autumn/Winter') feed which is high in potash.

'Bloom' formulations are ideal for *Phalaenopsis* or the flowering stages of other orchids, whereas 'Grow' formulations are ideal for the vegetative stages of most orchids, or *Phalaenopsis* when it is not in flower and so mostly nitrogen is needed.

To make it simple, if you have a small collection of different types of orchid, use a 'Grow' formulation for all orchids in spring and summer and a 'Bloom' formulation in the autumn and winter. If you only have a *Phalaenopsis* orchid, use a 'Bloom' formulation all year round.

Drip feeders may be popular and convenient, but the best way to feed an orchid is either by misting its leaves, roots and bark with a foliar feed (giving it humidity at the same time) or by using a concentrated fertiliser – or ideally a combination of the two.

Orchid roots take up nutrients better when they are moist, so if the orchid is very dry, water it a little while before applying a fertiliser solution.

Repotting

Orchids need regular repotting as they will outgrow their pots. If they are growing in bark this will need replacing, as it degrades over time. If you buy an orchid grown in sphagnum moss or coir (coconut fibres or dust that feels like soil) it is best to repot it into bark as soon as flowering stops.

Most orchids are best repotted after flowering in spring when new growth starts. See pages 23–48 for more information about repotting specific orchid types.

What is the best orchid growing medium?

It is crucial that orchids are repotted into a good-quality, graded bark specifically sold for orchids. In nurseries, where temperature, humidity, watering and light can be very closely monitored and regulated, orchids are grown in a variety of growing mediums. In a home environment, especially in the UK, the best medium by far is bark, as it drains and aerates well. Feel the bag before you buy any orchid bark – it should not feel heavy and you should be able to feel some chunkiness.

Soil, peat, 'bark-based' compost, or any 'compost' for that matter, is not suitable for orchids. These hold too much water and it is highly unlikely any orchid would survive in such a growing medium for long.

It is important not to overpot orchids. This means they should not be repotted in pots that are much larger than their root system. They need to dry out between watering, especially when growth is sluggish in winter, and a lot of bark will hold on to too much water.

Pots suitable for orchids

It is best to use transparent pots for all orchids, especially for *Phalaenopsis* (which are usually sold in clear pots anyway) as these enable the roots to photosynthesise and allow you to keep an eye on them as a guide for watering. As orchids tend to be top-heavy when in flower, it is a good idea to sit the clear pot in a larger, heavier ornamental pot. The roots should still get enough light.

Most other orchids types are sold in opaque pots because their roots are not as attractive as *Phalaenopsis* and they do not change colour significantly in response to watering.

The most crucial feature of any pot used for orchids is that it has adequate drainage – many large holes at the bottom – and that it provides the plant with good aeration. Most regular plastic plant pots are designed for plants grown in peat, so they have few small-sized drainage holes, which is not good for orchids. Use specific orchid pots with an air cone in the base to provide additional aeration.

This pot is ideal for orchids – it is transparent with plenty of drainage holes and an air cone for aeration.

You can use one large pot to plant several orchids together. Create an air cone by inserting a smaller pot upside down inside a larger one – this will help keep the growing medium well aerated and well drained. This shows a combination of a 9 cm pot inside a 21 cm pot, which would be good for three or four orchids.

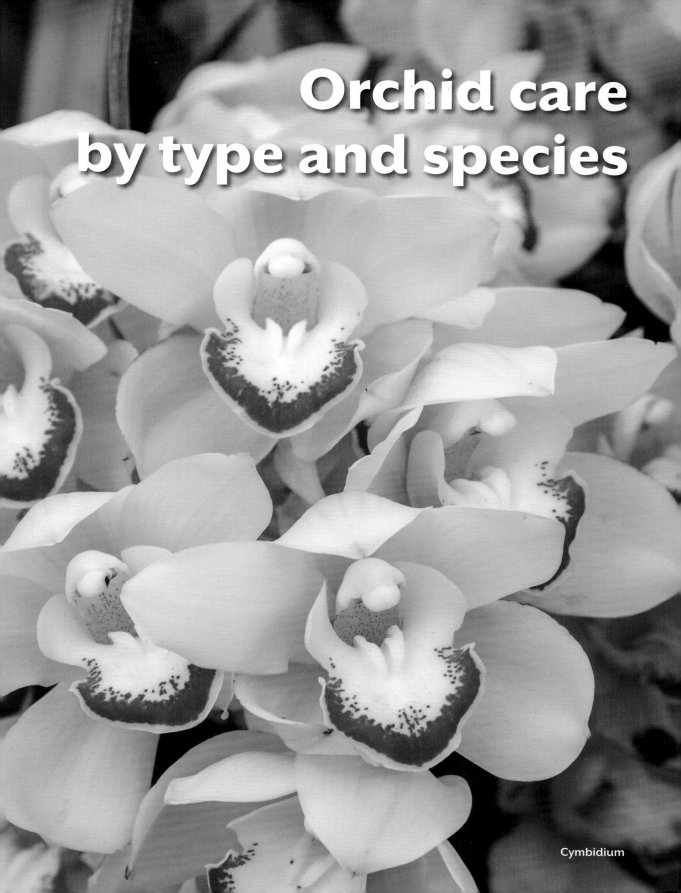

Orchid care by type and species

Cymbidium

Phalaenopsis

Phalaenopsis, which originate from South-East Asia, are the most popular orchids by far and are what most people think of when orchids are mentioned. They are very tolerant of a wide range of conditions, their flowers come in a huge variety of striking colours, and they will last for months. They are the perfect houseplants!

Temperature

Phalaenopsis are warm-growing orchids preferring a temperature range of 18–24°C (64–75°F). Providing the right temperature will not be a problem in an average house, but unheated spare rooms or conservatories are not really suitable for *Phalaenopsis* as they dislike large temperature fluctuations.

Windowsills next to double-glazed windows are the best place for them in winter, as cold air coming off a single-glazed window can be a problem. If your *Phalaenopsis* is on a windowsill with curtains that separate it from the warmth of the room when they are closed at night, move the plant on to a table near the window.

Light

Phalaenopsis will be damaged by full sun in the summer but will thrive in a sunny position in winter. South-facing windowsills are ideal in winter, but from early spring, move them out of direct sunlight either by using some kind of shading or by moving them to a north-, east- or west-facing windowsill. In the middle of the summer, when the sun is at its strongest, it is possible that even the direct light on an east-facing windowsill would be too much.

A large, bright, north-facing window with no blinds or curtains and no trees shading it is a good place for a *Phalaenopsis* in summer.

Signs of too much light

Even a moderate excess of light will cause leaves, particularly newer ones, to turn yellow. (Old leaves turn pale before they fall off and this is normal.)

If a leaf becomes overheated by sunlight, the exposed part dies and a white patch occurs. The damage around the dead part may turn black and become infected by bacteria. If this happens, cut the leaf back to healthy tissue.

Slight (left) and severe (above) direct sunlight damage on a Phalaenopsis *grown on a south-facing windowsill over the summer months.*

Signs of too little light

Depending on how little light a plant receives, it may not flower, it may not grow, and eventually it may lose its roots and die – though this could take years. If the plant grows it will be slowly and it will become 'leggy'. Inadequate light is the most common reason that *Phalaenopsis* orchids do not flower.

This plant has received the minimum light for growth and flowering. Many, green and large leaves are typical of low light conditions for most plants. This orchid will flower more frequently if it is moved to more light.

This Phalaenopsis *has the typical signs of growing in a very bright position (but no direct sunlight). Fewer, smaller, reddish, hard leaves are typical. Also, the leaves show early splitting due to low humidity. Although the plant will flower profusely, it is better to move it to a lower light position.*

Humidity

Although they can tolerate fairly low humidity, *Phalaenopsis* much prefer high humidity – when humidity is very low *Phalaenopsis* leaves tend to twist and split. Spray their leaves, and especially the roots and top of the bark, with water or a weak fertiliser solution at least two to three times a week. This is particularly important in winter when central heating dries the air.

Watering – root colour, weight

Allow the growing medium (bark) to dry out and the pot to become lighter between waterings. While the roots are green, the plant does not need watering but when the roots turn silver-white you need to water, especially if the pot feels light. If the roots are silver-white but the pot feels heavy, leave it and check again after a few days. The weight of the pot in combination with the colour of the roots is the most reliable guide to whether this type of orchid needs watering.

Feeding

To maintain long-term health and to promote healthy growth, feed your *Phalaenopsis* an appropriate liquid fertiliser. As *Phalaenopsis* grow and flower all year round, you can use a 'Bloom' type formulation (high in potash) throughout the year with every other watering.

Water the orchid beforehand to wet the roots, then water it with the diluted fertiliser solution.

A healthy, flowering Phalaenopsis *grown on a small humidity tray (a pot saucer and gravel).*

Signs of too much watering

- **Brown roots** – the odd brown or dead root inside the pot is fine but if there are many brown roots it is likely there is a problem, and the most likely cause is too frequent watering. If an orchid is watered too often the roots will become damaged, turn brown and rot (too much water in one go will not cause any damage, though). The roots will become mushy and only the internal threads will remain.
- **Floppy, wrinkly leaves** – a plant without roots can't replace the water it loses, so the leaves will dehydrate, become floppy and turn wrinkly.
- **Lots of aerial roots** – an orchid that is watered very frequently may also have too many aerial roots as it tries to find a less saturated environment. However, too many aerial roots can grow naturally if the orchid is not repotted regularly. Check to see how many healthy roots are inside the pot – if it is very few, the reason is likely to be overwatering.
- **Moss** – you may see moss growing inside or on the top of the bark.

Here there are no visible roots and the bark is very dark, which indicates that the plant has been watered very frequently and lost most of its roots. There are still a few roots, though, so the orchid should recover if the frequency of watering is adjusted.

Signs of too little watering

If a *Phalaenopsis* is not watered when the roots turn silver-white and the pot feels light (because the growing medium inside has started to dry), over time the roots will shrivel and some may flatten against the pot. Depending on the microclimate the orchid is in this can take several weeks to occur. If the plant becomes so short of water that the leaves become floppy and wrinkly or the roots become shrivelled, give the pot a good soak for 20–30 minutes.

Healthy, turgid, green roots. The root system is in great health and the orchid does not need watering.

Healthy, root system turning silver-white. Time to consider watering. Also water the orchid if the pot feels light.

Unhealthy, shrivelled, root system but recoverable. Dunk the pot in tepid water for 20–30 mins.

Flowering

Phalaenopsis are often sold with two or more flowering stems, but this is difficult to replicate at home where they tend to produce just one. However, a *Phalaenopsis* sold with branching flowering stems is likely to carry on producing branching flowering stems.

There are two options to encourage a *Phalaenopsis* to reflower:

1. *Phalaenopsis* can flower again on the same stem, so before all the flowers have died, and while the sap is still rising, cut the stem off about 1 cm above the third or fourth node (eye) depending on which one looks bigger. The node will then soon start to produce a side flowering stem. If the stem is cut after all the flowers have dropped it is less likely that this will happen. Some plants will produce side flowering stems naturally without the need to cut off the stem above a node.

Whether or not an orchid will produce a side flower stem depends on many factors such as the time of the year and how healthy the orchid is. The main factor, though, is whether the orchid is one that naturally produces branching flowering

Side flowering stem on a miniature Phalaenopsis.

A new shoot on an old flower spike, after it has been cut above a node.

stems – these are likely to have them when on display in the garden centre or nursery, so look out for them.

2. Wait until all the flowers drop off naturally, then cut off the stem at the base. The plant will make one or two new leaves before it produces the next flowering stem. The plant will take longer to flower again but you are likely to get more flowers on the stem.

When flowering finishes – especially if this happens during the summer – place the plant in a cool spot to encourage it to produce new flower spikes. After four to six weeks, move the plant back to normal warmer conditions.

If an orchid has two stems flowering at the same time, try the first method on the stronger stem and the second method on the other. The plant is more likely to reflower on the same stem if you try on only one of the stems.

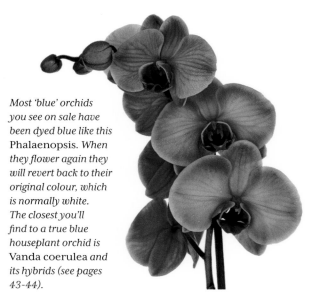

Most 'blue' orchids you see on sale have been dyed blue like this Phalaenopsis. *When they flower again they will revert back to their original colour, which is normally white. The closest you'll find to a true blue houseplant orchid is* Vanda coerulea *and its hybrids (see pages 43-44).*

Repotting

If you buy a *Phalaenopsis* in sphagnum moss or coir it is best to repot it into a bark mix as soon as it stops flowering because moss and coir degrade very quickly and hold too much water. If your orchid is already growing in bark it is best to repot 12–18 months after you buy it and every 18–24 months after that. The main reason for repotting an orchid is to replace the bark as it starts going mushy and holding too much water.

The best time for repotting is in spring or autumn when the plant is not in flower and the roots are actively growing (you'll see greenish or brownish tips at the end of the roots) but a healthy vigorous orchid can be repotted even when in flower – though it won't be as easy to handle.

Use a bark specifically for orchids and ideally a clear pot with adequate drainage and an air cone for aeration. Choose the size of the new pot carefully as it is easy to overpot an orchid. Look at the volume of the roots and aim for 50:50 roots and bark in the new pot. Usually you will need a new pot just one size larger than the old one, or a pot of the same size if you have had to remove a lot of dead roots. Typically, *Phalaenopsis* are sold in 12 cm pots, so for the first repotting use a 13 cm pot (or repot back into a 12 cm pot).

During repotting, fit all the aerial roots into the pot – this is easier if you slightly turn the orchid as you lower it. If there are too many unruly aerial roots, place the plant in tepid water for 10–15 minutes after you have removed the bark so the roots become more pliable. If this doesn't work and you have to 'break' the roots to put them in the pot, so be it. You are not breaking the actual root (which is a thread inside) but the velamen which will easily heal itself (see page 12). Remember – orchid roots are not your typical houseplant roots.

'Wild orchids' are closer to the original Phalaenopsis *and have many stems with smaller flowers. Avoid buying one with a flowering stem coming from between its top leaves (this applies to any orchid). This is where the orchid needs to make new leaves from. The 'wild orchid' is most commonly available in white but recently it became available in pink.*

The flowering stems of orchids (especially Phalaenopsis *) can be trained in many different shapes. If you want to try this with an orchid at home you need to be very careful and do it gradually as the flower stem develops. They snap easily.*

Miniature Phalaenopsis have smaller flowers but tend to be branching and very easy to reflower.

How to repot a *Phalaenopsis*

❶ *This* Phalaenopsis *is due for repotting, with many aerial roots and growing root tips. Prepare the orchid by watering it the day before or soaking in water for a few minutes before repotting, so the orchid will come free and the bark will be easy to remove.*

❷ *Take the orchid out of the pot by squeezing or even cutting off the old pot. Open up the roots and gently remove all the old growing medium. Rinse the roots in lukewarm water to wash out all the bark or moss pieces. Cut off any damaged or dead roots and dead flower stems with a sterile knife or scissors. If the orchid has a very vigorous root system, trim any lengthy roots to about 15 cm (6 in).*

❸ *All the bark and dead roots removed. This orchid had many dead roots at the bottom because it had been allowed to sit in water. A* Phalaenopsis *needs at least 10–12 good healthy-looking roots about 5–7.5 cm (2–3 in) long.*

❹ *Spray the aerial roots with foliar feed to make them more pliable, so you can fit them into the new pot.*

❺ *Place a thin layer (1–2 cm) of new bark in the bottom of the new pot. Lower the roots into the pot, holding the orchid in the centre of the pot with one hand with only the roots below the rim of the pot. Make sure all the roots are in the pot.*

❻ *Fill the spaces around the roots with new bark and shake the pot to ensure that all the spaces are filled. Water the orchid after repotting and then leave for a couple of weeks. You need to be careful with watering while the orchid gets established in the new pot – water sparingly until new roots develop.*

Repotting a neglected *Phalaenopsis*

1 *This* Phalaenopsis *has not been repotted for years so it has developed a long 'neck'. It is important that the aerial roots along the 'neck' are sprayed and kept healthy. Prepare the orchid as for general repotting (see opposite).*

2 *Take the orchid out of the pot, open up the roots and remove all the old bark.*

3 *Cut off the bottom part of the 'neck' making sure the remaining part has enough roots to support the plant – otherwise the bottom part should not be removed. Keeping the long 'neck' would mean you need to use a big pot with a lot of bark that will take a long time to drain.*

4 *Dust the cut with a little regular cinnamon powder – this will stop fungal diseases, such as wilting rot, and help to accelerate the plant's healing process.*

5 *A shorter 'neck' makes it easier to use an appropriately sized pot that drains well between watering. Make sure all the roots are in the pot.*

6 *Fill the spaces around the roots with new bark and shake the pot to ensure that all the spaces are filled. Water the orchid after repotting and then leave for a couple of weeks. You need to be careful with watering while the orchid gets established in the new pot – water sparingly until new roots develop.*

Cambria

Cambria-type orchids, often simply called Cambria, and also known as *Oncidium*, form a large group of hybrid orchids which have

beautiful, spotted, brightly coloured flowers. The group includes *Oncidium*, *Miltonia/Miltoniopsis* (pansy orchids), *Brassia* (spider orchids) and *Cochlioda*.

Cambria orchids have elongated pseudobulbs from which the leaves and long flower spikes develop. Pseudobulbs (pseudo is Greek for false) are modified stems, not true bulbs like onions. These orchids are very easy to look after and, given the right care, they will last for many years growing bigger each year with more flowering stems.

Temperature

Cambria orchids are cool-growing orchids with an ideal temperature range of 10–24°C (50–70°F), so make sure that they are not kept in a warm environment. Unheated spare rooms or windowsills away from radiators are ideal.

Light

Cambria orchids require bright conditions (with the exception of *Miltonia*). Like all orchids, they should not receive direct sunlight during the late spring and summer months. South-facing windowsills are ideal in winter (except for *Miltonia*). Position the plant with its new growth

Oncidium 'Mieke Von Holm' has a strong sweet smell, especially in the morning, and usually flowers in September and/or late winter.

facing the light to ensure it receives enough. An east- or west-facing windowsill is ideal when the sun starts to get stronger in the spring, or keep it there throughout the year.

Humidity

Cambria orchids require good humidity and respond well to spraying, especially during winter.

Watering

The thin roots of Cambria orchids are sensitive to too much or too little moisture, so aim for an even supply of water throughout the year, apart from in winter when they should be allowed to dry out a bit between waterings. Irregular watering may lead to concertina-like leaves.

Feeding

Cambria orchids require regular feeding. Use a 'Grow' type fertiliser all year round or, ideally, switch to a 'Bloom' formulation in the autumn and winter. This will help harden the pseudobulbs and improve flowering.

Flowering

Cambria orchid flowers will last for six to eight weeks, but they will not reflower on the same flowering stem. Once flowering has finished, carefully cut off the stem right at the base. This type of orchid will most commonly flower only once a year, in spring, but it is possible for them to flower twice a year if they are kept in a good growing environment. After flowering, these orchids need to develop good strong shoots before reflowering. These new shoots will grow into pseudobulbs, which will produce new flowers when they reach the size of the older pseudobulbs.

If the orchid does not flower again within a year, the most likely cause is excess warmth.

Occasionally remove any dead bases of leaves from around the pseudobulbs to encourage new roots to grow into the growing medium.

Repotting

As with all orchids, cambrias should be repotted every two years into a slightly larger pot. Do this in spring after flowering, when you can see new roots appearing.

Cambrias are normally sold in white pots – repot them into clear pots so you can see the root system. Any pot you use needs to have plenty of large holes for drainage and ideally an air cone in the base for aeration. Do not use an overly large pot as it will be difficult for the growing medium to drain properly.

Miltonia (pansy orchids) have soft, pale leaves and they are sensitive to direct sunlight. A north-facing windowsill or inside a bright room would be a good place to grow them at home.

2 Water the plant the day before so it is easy to remove from the pot. Remove the plant and tease away the old bark (or coir). Remove any old sheaths (dead bases of old leaves) or any old flower stems.

1 This Cambria is due for repotting as it is growing outside its pot. The plant is big enough to be divided if wished, but bigger plants produce bigger flower displays.

How to repot a Cambria orchid

3 Wash the roots, looking for any dead ones. If there are any, prune them off, retaining a good-sized root ball. Look for any old brown pseudobulbs and remove them. Don't remove any old pseudobulbs that are green, even if they have lost their leaves, as they are still useful to the plant, providing nourishment for new growth.

4 Place the plant in a suitably sized pot so there is sufficient room for two years' growth – approximately 2.5 cm (1 in) greater diameter.

Place a layer of bark mix in the base of the pot and hold the plant so that the base of the new growth is level with the rim of the pot. If not, adjust the level of the bark.

5 Hold the plant in place and pour in the bark mix. Firm it down and repeat until the pot is full. Water the orchid after repotting and then leave it for two weeks before you water again. Water sparingly while the plant gets established in its new pot.

The flowers of Cambria orchids come in all shapes and sizes and display magnificent colours, often very vibrant dark reds, purples and oranges, some speckled with white. Most species have a faint aroma, some have a strong one. Many of the orchids have branching flowering stems which gives a fuller and longer lasting flowering display. Cambrias are distinctive and easy to look after.

Oncidium *flowers come in very vibrant colours, in shades of yellow, red, white and pink. The petals and lip are often ruffled on the edges. The lip is enormous, partially blocking the small petals and sepals. Its name is derived from the Greek word 'onkos', meaning 'swelling'. This refers to the callus at the lower lip.*

Miltoniopsis *flowers are pansy-like. Showy, rounded and large, they are often fragrant and last for several weeks. Miltoniopsis are often sold with many flowering stems and will produce more every year.*

The scented Brassia *flowers have blackish-purple spots, and the white lips have distinctive green patches. This extra-terrestrial appearance makes* Brassia *flowers very eye-catching. The long ribbon-like flowers have earned the plant the nickname 'spider orchid'.*

Cattleya

Cattleya are among the most flamboyant orchids with large, beautiful, typically lilac-pink flowers. They originate from South America and can become quite large plants, but they are suitable for growing on a windowsill or in a conservatory in a warm, bright, airy location, and are relatively easy to look after. These orchids have a rest period in winter and flower in spring.

Temperature and light

These orchids require a temperature range of 16–24°C (61–75°F). During their rest period they can cope with night-time temperatures down to 12°C (54°F). They look like they can take a lot of light but they are in fact easily scorched in summer as their leaves are deceptively sensitive. East- or west-facing windowsills are best for cattleyas during spring and summer, but make sure they receive plenty of light in winter. If their leaves are dark green, sometimes with a gentle shade of red, this indicates they are receiving plenty of light. However, if their leaves are a pale green, they need to be moved to a brighter position.

Humidity and watering

Regular spraying (two to three times a week at least) will help with humidity throughout the year. Spray the pseudobulbs, roots and bark but avoid the leaves.

Cattleya need to be watered regularly during the growing season in spring and summer to encourage new growth, but must be given time to dry out between waterings in the autumn and winter.

Feeding

Cattleyas need more nutrients than the average orchid, so feed with a 'Grow' type fertiliser in every watering, apart from once a month when you should use water only. Make sure the growing medium is not too dry – use plain water first then water with the fertiliser solution.

Flowering

The flowers will last for three to four weeks on the plant or a couple of weeks as cut flowers. Sometimes the buds produce a sticky liquid just before blossoming – in the wild this is to attract ants that protect the plant from other insects, but in the home it can be a problem. Remove the sticky deposits with a cloth dipped in warm water or a dilute soap solution.

After flowering, remove the dead flowers and sheaths. The sheaths cover most of the pseudobulbs and removing them when they have withered will help the plant avoid being infested with scale insects.

Repotting

Cattleyas are best repotted every two years after flowering, like Cambria orchids (see page 34).

Cymbidium

These are magnificent orchids with large flowers and they are available in a fantastic range of colours. They will grow bigger every year with more flowering stems. They originate from high altitudes in the Himalayas where they grow as epiphytes on the branches of large trees or in well-drained soil. Provided they are not treated as normal houseplants, they are difficult to kill!

Temperature

Cymbidium orchids require temperatures of 10–20°C (50–68°F) and up to 30°C (86°F) in summer. Put them outside as soon as the danger of frost has passed and the night-time temperature does not fall below 10°C (50°F). Keep them outside for as long as possible in the autumn, and bring them indoors just before the first frosts. It is these low temperatures in late summer and autumn that will encourage the plant to produce flower stems. When you bring the orchid in from outside, dunk it in a bucket of water for about 10–20 minutes, so that any snails or insects that have found their way into the pot escape or drown, and wipe their leaves with plant wipes to remove any pests. Also, take this opportunity to remove any dead bases of leaves from around the pseudobulbs. These are the coolest-growing orchids and should be grown in the coolest room of the house (or a heated conservatory) in a position that receives good light. Bring them into

the main part of your house only when flower buds start to open to enjoy their fantastic display.

Light

Cymbidium orchids require plenty of light all year round. An east- or west-facing position where they receive some sun in the morning or afternoon is ideal, but if you see the foliage starting to yellow, move it to a shadier position.

Watering

Keep them moist but not wet in the summer but allow them to dry more between waterings in the autumn and winter. Water thoroughly from the top or, if the pot is very solid with roots and watering from the top is difficult, dunk in water for 10–20 minutes. It is important to regularly check the plant in the summer when it is outside, as dry spells combined with wind and sun can dry them out. If it rains a lot in summer it is best to move them to a covered spot, so the pot does not become waterlogged.

Humidity

Cymbidium orchids thrive in high humidity, so it's a good idea to spray them regularly with a foliar feed. This has two other advantages: it helps satisfy their high nutrient requirements and keeps red spider mites away.

Feeding

Cymbidium orchids need a lot of feed, especially during the growing season, so use an orchid

Repotting a *Cymbidium*

❶ Water the plant the day before so it is easy to remove from the pot. Remove the plant from its pot, prune any dead roots and remove the old bark, retaining a root ball of good size.

❷ Look for old brown pseudobulbs and remove them. Don't remove any pseudobulbs that are still green. Remove any old sheaths (dead bases of old leaves) or any old flower stems.

❸ Choose a larger pot so there is sufficient room for two years' growth – about 2.5–5 cm (1–2 in) larger in diameter should be fine. Place a layer of bark at the bottom and stand the plant so that the base of the new growth is level with the rim of the pot.

❹ Hold the plant in the middle and add bark mix. Tap the pot down to ensure that there are no gaps in the bark mix and repeat until the pot is full. Water the plant immediately and thereafter sparingly while the plant gets established in its new pot.

Potting on

This *Cymbidium* was due for repotting as it was sitting proud of the pot.

The root system is very healthy and the bark has not degraded much, so it is potted on to a larger pot as in steps 3 and 4 above.

Dividing a *Cymbidium*

When a plant gets very large you can divide it (but you don't have to if you enjoy large plants). It needs to be large enough so that every new plant will have four or five healthy pseudobulbs and a new growth.

Feel the plant and look for a natural adjoining point to cut, so that you have at least five pseudobulbs in each plant. Sprinkle a bit of cinnamon powder on the wound to prevent any infection.

This miniature Cymbidium *can be divided as it has about twenty pseudobulbs and five new shoots.*

The bark is removed and the plant is divided into three at natural dividing points.

Three new and rejuvenated miniature Cymbidium *orchids.*

Flower spikes develop on Cymbidium *orchids in late autumn or early winter.*

fertiliser at four times the recommended dose with every other watering. Use a 'Grow' type fertiliser all year round, or ideally switch to a 'Bloom' formulation for autumn and winter. This will help to harden the pseudobulbs and improve flowering.

Repotting

Repot cymbidiums every two to three years, in spring after flowering. Cymbidiums grow sideways so make sure that there is room in the pot for a couple of years' growth.

The plant will 'tell' you when it needs repotting. It either pushes itself up in the pot due to the volume of roots at the bottom, or grows to the edge of the pot.

As plants grow bigger, you can divide them when the plant has at least ten healthy green pseudobulbs and two new growths – every new plant should have at least five pseudobulbs to support the new growth.

An alternative to repotting (where you remove the old bark and trim back the roots) is to simply lift it into a larger pot and add extra bark. This is known as 'dropping on' and is done when the roots are healthy and the old bark has not degraded much.

Dendrobium

Dendrobium phalaenopsis

There are two types of *Dendrobium* orchids, both requiring different care.

Dendrobium nobile (bamboo cane orchids) produce short flower spikes alongside the cane-like stems. They are popular orchids with long knobbly canes which are, in fact, long joined pseudobulbs that bear long-lasting, waxy, fragrant flowers, usually white or lilac. These orchids have a definite growing and resting period and, as long as you can recognise this and adapt your care, they should be easy to look after and produce amazing flowering displays every year. Because of the need for cool temperatures during their rest period, *D. nobile* are sometimes called cool-growing dendrobiums.

Dendrobium phalaenopsis is one of the easiest orchids to grow. Often called warm-growing dendrobiums, they have smaller canes than *D. nobile* and long flower spikes from the top of the cane. *D. phalaenopsis* produce one to four flower spikes per pseudobulb with two to eight flowers per spike. They are sold in a variety of colours including violet, lilac, magenta, white and purplish blue. Over time they will grow to be large plants and it is not uncommon to see plants with 50 or so canes. If a plant has more than ten canes it can be divided, but it is not necessary.

Temperature – cool-growing dendrobiums

Buy *Dendrobium nobile* orchids in spring rather than autumn so their temperature requirements coincide with the seasons, otherwise the seasons and weather will be against you. A plant bought in spring can be placed on an east- or west-facing windowsill to receive plenty of light for its growing phase.

From the formation of the buds in late winter and during spring and summer when the orchid is in its growing phase, these orchids can be kept in warm conditions. The buds will develop to flowers and soon new shoots will emerge from the bottom of the plant. At the end of the summer, when the new canes are fully developed and are almost the height of the old ones, the orchid will go into rest and it needs to be moved somewhere cooler with minimum temperatures of about 10°C (50°F). A frost-free conservatory or an unheated spare room is ideal until new buds have formed again.

Temperature – warm-growing dendrobiums

D. phalaenopsis have similar temperature requirements to *Phalaenopsis* – place them in a warm room where the temperature does not drop below 15°C (59°F).

Light

Both *Dendrobium* orchids need a bright position, especially in the winter, so a south-facing windowsill would be ideal. Like other orchids, they do not like much direct sunlight in spring and summer.

Humidity

These orchids respond well to higher humidity, so spray the plants and substrate regularly with soft water or rainwater, or sit them on a humidity tray (see page 20). Ideally, also spray with a foliar feed fertiliser.

Watering

Dendrobium phalaenopsis and *D. nobile* need regular watering to keep the growing medium moist, but not saturated, during their growing phase in spring and summer. *D. phalaenopsis* grow slowly in the winter months, so you need to water a bit less. *D. nobile*, on the other hand, is normally in rest in autumn and winter, so water sparingly and spray regularly with soft water or rainwater.

Emerging new growth on Dendrobium nobile. *The top roots are damaged due to exposure to sunlight and possibly from using a fertiliser containing urea. It would be good to repot this plant, so its roots are not exposed and the roots from the new growth go into bark.*

Developing canes on Dendrobium nobile.

They still require plenty of light but water sparingly until you see buds forming on the new canes, which will be around January or February. You can then resume normal watering.

Feeding

Feed dendrobiums with a 'Grow' type fertiliser throughout the year with every other watering. They will also benefit from a 'Bloom' type feed while the buds are developing in winter and early spring.

Dendrobium nobile

Flowering

Dendrobium nobile will flower once a year but *D. phalaenopsis* can easily flower more. After flowering it is important not to cut off the old canes as these contain water and nutrients that will benefit the new growth. The old flowering canes will last for many years, so you only need to remove them when they become diseased or turn yellow and wrinkly.

The key to good flowering for *D. nobile* is the three to four month period of cool temperatures and dry growing medium after the growing phase. If they are not given this treatment they will produce many new plantlets ('keikis') instead of flowers. Support any new canes with sticks to ensure they grow straight upwards and to stop them falling sideways as they become top-heavy.

For *D. phalaenopsis* no special treatment is required for good flowering, but they do need a bright environment to produce abundant flowers. In contrast to the cool-growing types, *D. phalaenopsis* will commonly reflower on old canes.

Repotting

Both dendrobiums generally need repotting every two years into a slightly larger pot – resist the urge to overpot them as good drainage is essential. Repot as for cambrias (see page 34).

There are two types of Dendrobium phalaenopsis: Dendrobium kingianum *type (right) with many smaller canes and smaller flowers, and* Dendrobium Emma or Sha-nook (above) *with fewer but larger canes and flowers. They both require similar growing conditions but* D. kingianum *will benefit from slightly cooler and drier conditions in the winter (nowhere near the requirements of* D. nobile*). They are both very easy to grow and reflower at home. Over time they will become bigger plants with more flowers.*

Vanda

Warm-growing, light-loving plants, *Vanda* orchids are heavy feeders, too. These orchids, native to South-East Asia, are usually sold bare-rooted – which is how they grow in the wild, humid forests – sometimes in tall vases, because of their visually attractive long roots.

Temperature, light and humidity

They like a temperature range of 18–25°C (64–77°F) and can be kept outdoors in southern areas of the UK in July and August, when they will also benefit from the higher humidity and summer rain. They will do well in a shady conservatory with a bucket of water underneath them for added humidity, but move to a south-facing windowsill in the winter to let the maximum sunlight available reach the plant.

Flowering

Most commonly sold hybrids have blue, pink or orange flowers, but more colours come on to the market each year. Given the right environment

Extract from *Vanda coerulea* flowers has been used to create eyedrops for treating glaucoma and cataracts.

with high temperatures and light, a *Vanda* can reflower, often with flowers lasting four to six weeks.

Repotting a bare-rooted Vanda

At home it is easier to grow them potted up into bark which will help to keep a humid environment around the roots.

The best time to pot a *Vanda* is in the spring after flowering and when you can see the roots actively growing. Use a clear pot of the appropriate size with plenty of large

drainage holes. Prepare the orchid by immersing its roots in water for 20–30 minutes so they are malleable. Cut off any damaged or dead roots and flower stems, and trim any lengthy roots to about 50–60 cm (20–25 in). Place a 2.5 cm (1 in) layer of new bark at the bottom of the new pot.

Hold the plant so that its base is below the rim of the pot. Twisting the plant will make it easier to fit all the roots in the pot. If this does not work and you have to break the roots to put them in the pot, it's okay. You are not breaking the actual root (which is a thread inside) but the spongy layer around them which can easily heal itself. Hold the plant in place and add bark mix. Firm down and repeat until the pot is full. Water the orchid after repotting and resume normal watering after few days. Repot as for *Phalaenopsis* (they are closely related) every two to three years.

If you grow your Vanda *bare-rooted, you need to spray it heavily with soft, tepid water. During the winter you will need to spray the plant (especially the roots) every two to three days, increasing the frequency to daily as summer approaches. Use a weak foliar feed every two to three sprayings. You can reduce the amount of spraying – and the risk of the plant getting dehydrated – if you dip the roots in water regularly. The more dippings, the less spraying. Alternate a 'Bloom' type fertiliser solution with plain water.*

If you have potted up your Vanda, *you can water it freely. Use the weight of the pot as a guide to whether this type of orchid needs watering, as* Vanda *roots tend to stay green even if they are on the dry side. Ensure the plant dries out a bit between waterings, but not as much as* Phalaenopsis. *They may need watering two to three times a week in the hot summer but less in the winter.* Vanda *require more food than the average orchid. Use a 'Bloom' type fertiliser every week, apart from once a month when you should just use water. When potted in bark,* Vanda *is likely to produce aerial roots outside the pot, which is not a problem. Just spray them regularly.*

If you keep your Vanda *in a tall glass vase you will need to fill the vase with just enough water to cover all the roots, but not the actual plant, and leave it for 20–30 minutes. It is very important that you use soft water or rainwater at room temperature. Water this way two to three times a week and leave a bit of water at the bottom, perhaps with some pebbles so the roots are not in the water. This will create some added humidity. Alternate a 'Bloom' type fertiliser solution with plain water. Feel free to spray the plant and its roots in the vase regularly, with a weak foliar feed.*

Paphiopedilum

Paphiopedilum (slipper orchids) originate from many parts of the world, from the Himalayas in Asia to the Pacific islands, and from sea level up to 2,700 m (8,800 ft). In their natural habitat, they normally grow on the forest floor among the humus (leaf mould) and decomposing vegetation. They will flower once a year for about two to three months and some varieties, such as *Paphiopedilum* 'Pinocchio', have four to six flowers on each stem, which will flower in succession.

Temperature and light

Most slipper orchids sold in the UK require an ideal temperature range of 16–21°C (61–70°F). A good spot for them would be a north-facing windowsill away from any radiators, which dry out the air around them. Alternatively, they can be grown away from a windowsill in a bright room.

Watering

These orchids should never be allowed to dry out. They require a moist, but not wet, growing medium. Use tepid soft water or rainwater as these orchids are more sensitive to water quality and temperature than other orchids, and take care that water does not go between the leaves or into the centre of the plant. If this happens, use some tissue to soak it up (you may have to twist the tissue to ensure that it reaches into the centre of the orchid). Do not mist their leaves.

Feeding

Use a 'Grow' type fertiliser at half the recommended strength with every other watering throughout the year.

Repotting

Paphiopedilum orchids need to be repotted every other year, often into the same sized pot as it is important that these orchids are not overpotted – this would lead to a wet, or even oversaturated, growing medium. Small grade bark is the best medium to grow them in at home. Divide these orchids if they naturally come apart during repotting and pot them into the same size or smaller pots. Take care not to damage any tissue during repotting as *Paphiopedilum* are susceptible to rot. If any wounds occur, sprinkle with cinnamon powder to prevent fungal infection.

Zygopetalum

Native to high mountain slopes and ridges in South America, *Zygopetalum* orchids are terrestrial orchids that grow in wet, shady sites among rocks. They have ovoid pseudobulbs and can easily grow to become big plants. The most commonly sold hybrid in the UK is called 'Sensation' and is normally sold in late spring and summer.

Temperature, light and humidity

These are cool-growing orchids and they appreciate cool night-time temperatures all the way down to 12°C (54°F). They cope with a larger fluctuation of temperature between day and night than other orchids, but can be damaged easily by direct sunlight in the spring and summer, so ideally they should be grown on an east-facing windowsill.

They grow best in a humid environment, but do not spray the leaves as water can accumulate in the core of the plant and lead to rot. Instead, sit the orchid on a humidity tray.

Watering, feeding and repotting

Water thoroughly from the top, ideally in the morning so that any foliage that gets wet has time to dry before temperatures drop at night. Feed regularly with every other watering with a 'Grow' formulation during the growing season. They should be repotted in the same way as Cambria-type orchids – see page 34 for details.

Flowering

Zygopetalum usually flower once a year but sometimes flower again within the year. Temperature fluctuations and cool nights will help with flowering. Their flowers are scented, very striking and unusually coloured purple and green.

Masdevallia

Masdevallia are native to the American tropics where their natural habitats are tropical humid or wet forests at high altitudes. With a few exceptions, they are pollinated by flies. Often referred to as 'kite orchids', *Masdevallia* require a cool, humid and airy environment. They can be temperamental and difficult to bring into bloom, but their distinguished flowers are worth the effort.

Temperature and light

The *Masdevallia* orchids most commonly sold as houseplants grow within an ideal temperature range of 10–20°C (50–64°F), and do not require particularly bright conditions. Ideal spots for them in the home would be in a spare room, a bathroom, a north-facing windowsill, or further inside a room.

Humidity, watering and feeding

Water well and keep the growing medium damp throughout the year. This orchid does not need to dry out between waterings. Spray the orchid regularly to ensure it is kept moist or use a humidity tray.

Use a 'Grow' type fertiliser once to twice a month at half the recommended strength for normal orchids throughout the year.

Repotting

They are normally sold potted in moss. When you repot the orchid, remove the old moss but ensure you don't disturb the roots too much. Repot into a mix of two parts moss, one part perlite and one part bark. Repot every two years and avoid overpotting (don't repot in a pot much larger than their root system).

Masdevallia *orchids will respond well to the extra humidity provided by a humidity tray.*

Ludisia

Commonly known as the 'jewel orchid', *Ludisia discolor* is native to South-East Asia where it normally grows in evergreen lowland forests in shade, often near streams. It is a terrestrial orchid, but often grows on rocky substrates. *Ludisia* is appreciated for its velvety, attractively coloured leaves rather than its numerous flowers (which are small and white). Individual flowers last for two to three weeks, and the inflorescence for two to three months. In the wild, the white flowers attract a butterfly that drinks from a nectar cavity at the base of the lip.

Temperature and light

This is a warm-growing orchid, but at very warm temperatures it can become 'leggy', especially if the light is not very bright. It is more sensitive to direct light than most other orchids, and prolonged time in direct sunlight can scorch and discolour its leaves. It is best placed on a north-facing windowsill, or inside rooms out of direct light.

Watering and feeding

Water this orchid from the top of the growing medium and ensure it can drain thoroughly. You should allow the medium to dry out completely before watering again as the fleshy stems are susceptible to rot. Do not spray the leaves – this may cause marks or discoloration. Use a 'Grow' type fertiliser with every other watering throughout the year.

Repotting

Ludisia orchids need repotting every two years, ideally after flowering. Use bark, ideally with 10–20 per cent sphagnum moss to increase moisture retention. The stems grow sideways and they can occasionally break off. If this happens, plant the broken stem in moss, water thoroughly and leave in a shady place for at least six weeks, until roots start to develop. When the roots are well developed, plant in a small shallow pot.

Although Ludisia *discolor orchids are mainly appreciated for their leaves, their flowers are pretty too.*

Pests and diseases

Mealybug on a Phalaenopsis

There are not many pests or diseases that affect orchids in the home, but a few do, especially mealybugs and scale insects. It is good to inspect your plants carefully from time to time, especially in early summer. If you do spot any insects or disease symptoms on an orchid, isolate and treat the plant immediately to prevent other plants getting infected.

Mealybugs

There are many types of mealybug (Pseudococcidae). These sap-sucking insects are white and appear fluffy, like cotton wool, and are 1–5 mm in size. Their activity and growth depend on the temperature – the higher the temperature, the faster they multiply. Mealybugs suck sap from the plant causing distortion, yellowing and loss of leaves. They produce honeydew that can become infected with sooty mould. Their presence is often accompanied by ants which feed on the honeydew. Mealybugs can enter the home from outside, come from other houseplants, or they may already be on the

Mealybug infestation on Dendrobium nobile; *they have a fondness for the softer parts of the plant.*

Early signs of mealybugs on a Phalaenopsis *leaf.*

plant or in the growing medium when you buy it (but may not be visible or very active due to the temperature). The first sign of their presence is a cotton-wool-like mass on the leaves or other soft parts of the plant. These are mealybug eggs and if you take no action you will soon see live adults appear. Mealybugs often hide in the crevices of plants, where the leaves meet the stem and at the base, or on the backs of the flowers. They can also hide in the bark inside the pot, or any other nooks and crannies around the plant.

If you spot any mealybugs, use a cotton bud dipped in alcohol to remove the pests and clean the ornamental pot and the windowsill area around the plant with dilute bleach.

You can use a general houseplant insecticide – follow the safety instructions on the product label. Alternatively, you can use a contact insecticide or horticultural soap – both are safe to use inside the home especially if you have pets or children. Horticultural soap will break down the greasy covering of the bug, which makes it vulnerable and kills it. Most contact insecticides will cover the bug in a fatty substance which suffocates it. In both cases you will need to spray the entire plant to make sure you reach all the bugs. As both horticultural soaps and contact insecticides do not normally kill eggs, you will need to spray at least four times (once every four days) to deal with the problem.

If the plant has a heavy mealybug infestation, cut off and discard any heavily infected parts (flowers, stems etc.), before you treated. If you can see insects in the bark, it is best to take the plant out of the pot and remove all the bark you can. Keep the plant in a polythene bag (to maintain humidity) while you treat it with insecticide and then repot it in fresh bark after you have killed all the insects.

Mites

Despite their name, red spider mites (*Tetranychus urticae*) are not usually red, nor are they spiders, but they do make webs. They are extremely small, just about visible to the naked eye. Red spider mites are greenish-yellow (apart from in autumn when they turn deep red), wingless, eight-legged creatures, with a dark spot on each side of their bodies. They tend to attack mostly *Cymbidium*, *Dendrobium* and Cambria orchids. They will initially attack the underside of the leaves, which turn silver-grey, and then the buds and flowers. In dry, warm conditions they can multiply very quickly and can severely weaken and disfigure plants. They remove sap and chlorophyll from the plant, which results in the characteristic blanched, silvery appearance of the leaf, and their sapsucking can also cause bruised-looking areas on flowers.

False spider mites, or phalaenopsis mites (*Tenuipalpus pacificus*), tend to attack *Phalaenopsis* orchids and do not spin webs. They cause dark spots on both the tops and undersides of leaves, eventually killing the leaf tissue. False spider mites have a slow development, with a life cycle

of at least 64 days. Mites are quite often vectors of diseases so it is important to get rid of them as soon as you notice any.

A good way to tell if you have mites is to wipe a white cloth or tissue over both sides of a leaf. If mites or their eggs are present, you will see reddish or brownish streaks on the cloth. Another test is to tap a leaf over a piece of white paper – watch to see if any of the dislodged particles that fall on to the paper move (use a magnifying glass, as mites are often barely visible to the naked eye).

The best prevention and control is to provide the orchid with the correct humidity. Regular misting and spraying (especially on the underside of the leaves) will prevent attacks and control the problem if it occurs.

If there is an infestation, treat like mealybugs.

Scale insects

There are many different species of scale insect which can be divided into two different families; soft scales (Coccidae) and hard scales (Diaspididae). Scale insects often look like small bumps on the stems and undersides of the leaves. Some are black, some brown, some are hard and others are quite soft. Some types will attach themselves to a specific type of orchid, whereas others will attack many orchid types. Scale insects are very fond of *Cattleya* and *Phalaenopsis* orchids where they will attack the leaf tops and undersides, as well as the flowers.

If there is an infestation, treat like mealybugs.

Scale insects on a white Phalaenopsis *flower (below) and a* Cymbidium *leaf (below right).*

Green aphid with live young.

Diseases and viruses

Orchids growing in the home will not often suffer from fungal or bacterial diseases, which are a sign of poor growing conditions. These can occur, though, if orchids are grown at low temperatures combined with too much moisture, such as in conservatories or on cold windowsills where the air does not circulate well. As with all houseplants, low temperatures should be accompanied by a dry atmosphere, and warm temperatures with high humidity.

Viruses are difficult to diagnose at home so are beyond the scope of this book. If your orchid has pale or unpigmented patches, patterning or discolorations on the leaves or flowers, it could be a viral infection. By far the most common of the 25 viruses that affect orchids, are the cymbidium mosaic virus (CymMV) and odontoglossum ringspot virus (ORSV). They create a mosaic-type pattern or ring-like markings respectively. Viruses are not curable so the best thing is to isolate and dispose of the affected plant. Visual clues alone are not enough to detect a virus and you can find further information on testing for orchid viruses at www.aos.org/AOS?media/content-images/PDFs/Detecting_Virus.pdf

Prevention is better than cure, so regularly wipe the leaves with a plant wipe or a damp cloth dipped in very dilute soapy water. As well as removing dust and allowing the leaves to photosynthesise more effectively, a regular clean will remove any pests before they get a hold on the plant.

Aphids

Aphids (Aphidoidea) are a group of sap-sucking insects which includes greenfly, whitefly and blackfly. They will attack the softer parts of the plant, such as the new buds, and excrete a sticky honeydew which will soon become infected with a sooty mould. Although the damage may be difficult to see at first, as the affected parts spread it will become more apparent – affected buds will be disfigured and they are very likely to drop. Aphids are easy to spot and their presence is often accompanied by ants, which milk aphids for their honeydew.

If there is an infestation, treat like mealybugs.

Common questions and answers

Cambria (Oncidium)

Why is my orchid not flowering?

Phalaenopsis

Low light is by far the most likely reason your plant is not flowering, so it's best to address this issue first. If a healthy *Phalaenopsis* has not flowered for a long time, say nine months or so, it is mostly likely not receiving enough light in its current position. Another sign that low light is a problem is if the most recent leaves of the plant are larger than the previous ones, especially if they are floppy. Encourage the plant to flower by moving it to a brighter position.

Another reason your orchid may not be flowering is room temperature. *Phalaenopsis* orchids should ideally be kept between 18–24°C (65–75°F). If the orchid has been kept in a room that is regularly warmer than this, try moving it to a cooler room, but one that does not drop below 15°C (59°F), for about four to six weeks, before moving it back to its original position (unless, of course, this position also receives little light).

For more information on ideal *Phalaenopsis* growing conditions see pages 24–31.

Cambria-type orchids

Unlike *Phalaenopsis*, the most likely reason a Cambria-type orchid will not flower is that it is being kept in conditions that are too warm for it. Move it to a cooler position with a daytime temperature no higher than 22°C (72°F) and a night-time temperature no lower than 10°C (50°F). A new pseudobulb will flower when it grows to about the same size as the old ones. For more information on ideal Cambria growing conditions see page 32.

Cymbidium orchids

If your *Cymbidium* orchid has not flowered for 12 months, the likely causes are insufficient fertiliser, not enough light or, most likely, an insufficiently long period of low temperatures. If a *Cymbidium* orchid is kept indoors continuously, the relatively warm temperatures and relatively low light will prevent it from flowering or growing vigorously, and it will eventually wither and die.

To enjoy plenty of striking flowers, move the plant outdoors in spring (after the danger of frost has passed) to a sheltered position where it will receive good (but indirect) sunlight. Feed it well and the plant should produce plenty of flowers in late autumn or early winter depending on the variety. For more information on ideal *Cymbidium* growing conditions see page 37.

Why are my orchid's leaves concertina-like?

This can occasionally happen with Cambria orchids and is not a big problem. It is due to irregular watering – the plant gets too dry and then gets too wet and the growing leaf starts and stops in response to the available water, hence the concertina effect. This can be prevented by regular watering according to the needs of the plant.

Concertina leaves on a Cambria-type orchid.

Why does my orchid flower continuously?

It is not uncommon for *Phalaenopsis* to flower non-stop. Given the right conditions, some hybrids will flower profusely with very little time between producing flowering stems, if any time at all. Continuous flowering may be desirable, but it can exhaust the plant. To prevent this, feed the plant regularly with a 'Grow' type formulation to support vegetative growth and direct the plant towards making new leaves and keeping the current leaves in good condition, rather than flowering. If your plant looks 'tired' and has not produced new leaves in a long time, it is worth considering cutting off the flower stems as soon as the flowers start to fade to give the plant time to recover.

What are the small brown raised spots on the leaves, stem or flowers of my orchid?

Raised spots are most likely brown scale insects – limpet-like insects that feed by sucking sap. See page 51 for more information on prevention and treatment.

Scale insects on a Phalaenopsis *stem*

Why have the leaves on my *Phalaenopsis* shrivelled up?

This is usually because the plant cannot take up any water, either because it is too dry or it has lost most of its roots due to overwatering.

Check the roots carefully. If you can see plenty of roots through the pot but they are shrivelled and silver-white, the likely cause is lack of water. Give the plant plenty of tepid water and spray it regularly. Alternatively dunk it in tepid water for 20–30 minutes. Adjust future waterings accordingly, so you don't let the plant get too dry. If the top leaves (the newest ones) are shrivelled, the plant may not recover, but it is always worth a try.

If the roots inside the pot are brown and mushy, or you cannot see many roots at all, then the likely cause is overwatering which has damaged the roots to the point that the plant cannot take up any water. Do not

water the plant for a while but spray it regularly, ideally with a foliar feed. Only when you can see new roots developing should you give the plant some water, and even then give it just a little to maintain moisture around the roots.

Alternatively, put the plant into a transparent polythene bag to keep the humidity high. Spray occasionally until you see signs of new roots, when you can pot it up and water sparingly.

Why does my orchid have yellow or red buds that don't open and then fall off? -or- Why did all the flowers on my orchid fade at the same time?

This problem can occur with all orchids. Bud drop is the result of an environmental shock, such as a period of very low light or darkness, cold or drought. If you have bought the plant in the last two to three weeks, it is unlikely to be something you have done – the likely cause is that during transport from the nursery to the garden centre, or while at the garden centre, the plant got too dry, was exposed to a long period of cold or darkness, or a combination of all three.

Orchids are slow-reacting plants and by the time you see a problem there is often little you can do apart from trying to work out the conditions that led to this problem and avoid them in future.

It is important to check the colour of the flower buds when you buy a plant. Look for healthy green buds or buds that are taking on the colour of the flower coming through.

If the plant has been in your home for over

Avoid buying plants with yellow or reddish buds.

a month, again, the cause is one of the three factors above. Dryness, or a cold draught, is more likely to be the problem than a long dark period, unless you've had a spell of very dark winter weather. Is the orchid near a window that you leave open during cold weather? Did it get too dry between watering? Check and adjust the growing environment. The damaged buds will not come back to health, but you can prevent future problems.

Flowering should come to an end gradually, and flowers should fade in the order they opened. If they all fade or dry at the same time it indicates a possible problem – most likely the plant got too dry (see page 64).

Why have the pseudobulbs on my orchid shrivelled up?

Some shrivelling, especially on old pseudobulbs, is normal and some Cambria-type orchids have naturally shrivelled pseudobulbs. If you bought your orchid with healthy, green, turgid pseudobulbs and they have subsequently shrivelled, then this is because the plant cannot take up any water.

If the roots are dry and the pot feels very light, it is the result of severe underwatering. Water the plant, spray regularly and adjust future waterings.

If the roots are brown and mushy, the likely cause is overwatering, which has damaged the roots so the plant cannot take up water. Do not water the plant until the bark dries out and thereafter water sparingly until you see new

roots develop. Adjust future waterings.

Orchids with pseudobulbs, unlike *Phalaenopsis*, are more likely to recover as they have a reservoir of nutrients and water in the pseudobulbs (which is getting low, hence the shrivelling).

Why have the tips of the roots turned brown or black, or become threads?

Before you put your orchid back into its ornamental pot after watering you need to make sure it has drained completely so the lower roots do not end up sitting in water. This is especially important if the ornamental pot has a flat bottom. If it ends up sitting in water, the tips of the roots at the bottom of the pot will rot and turn from a healthy green to brown or black, and in time they will rot back to the central thread.

Why are my orchid's roots spilling out of its pot?

In the case of *Phalaenopsis*, it is quite natural for some roots to grow outside the pot over time and this is nothing to worry about. It is a good idea to spray them with water, or with a foliar feed, so they stay healthy and don't wither, turn brown and die. You can tuck them into the pot when you next repot the plant.

If there are lots of roots outside the pot, and the roots inside the pot look healthy, the plant is ready to be repotted. (*Phalaenopsis* need repotting every 18–24 months.)

If there are lots of new roots outside the pot, but the roots inside look brown or sparse, it is likely that the environment inside the pot is too wet for the orchid, so the plant is sending all its new roots outside – it is suffocating inside the pot and trying to get some air outside. Wait for the growing medium inside the pot to dry out before you water again and adjust the frequency of future waterings. It is unlikely the brown roots will come back, but you will save the plant and in time new roots will grow inside the pot. Alternatively, repot the plant and adjust the frequency of future waterings.

For orchids with pseudobulbs, as soon as a few roots start growing outside the pot – or much better, if they are just about to – it means the plant needs repotting. See pages 30–31.

Phalaenopsis with flower stem and growing aerial roots.

Why has a small plant appeared on one of the flowering stems/canes?

It not rare for a small plant to grow on the flowering stem of a *Phalaenopsis* – it is not related to any environmental conditions. The small

plant is called a 'keiki' (Hawaiian for baby) and you can deal with it in two ways. You can either snap it off from the stem and discard it (to prevent it weakening the parent plant and delaying its next flowering) or you can nurture it as a small plant.

Spray the keiki's roots with a foliar feed every day for its nourishment and root vigour. When it has four or five roots about 5 cm (2 in) long, you can cut about 1 cm (1/2 in) of the surrounding stem from the mother plant to detach it, then pot it up in bark in a small pot. Water it carefully as it has only a few roots, and mist it regularly with a foliar feed for nourishment and humidity. It will probably take a few years to come to flower, but it will grow to be an exact copy of the parent plant.

Keikis can also grow on *Dendrobium nobile*, as a response to the orchid not having a rest period in cool, dry conditions when the new canes have matured, so it grows keikis rather than flowers. You can treat the keikis the same way as for those on *Phalaenopsis*, spraying them until they have enough good roots, but you can just snap them off the cane, rather than cutting a bit of the cane off with the keiki. Pot three or four of them together in a small pot and grow them on to become bigger plants (see pages 40–42 on care of *D. nobile*).

Keikis can often appear on *Dendrobium phalaenopsis* (the *D. kingianum* type). They will not stop the plant from flowering, and they can be treated the same way.

The keikis on this Dendrobium *are ready to be snapped and potted on. You can then grow the plant to produce new canes.*

I see small black flies appearing from the compost. What shall I do?

These are likely to be fungus gnats (Sciaridae). They are very small and slender, mosquito-like flies. Unless you keep your orchid very wet, they would only possibly appear if you use a wet repotting mix which contains the eggs already. They hatch when in warm home conditions. It is very unlikely to happen if you use a good quality bark repotting mix. The older the potting medium is, the more likely it is to be infested with gnat larvae.

Gnats and their larvae are not harmful to orchids. They should disperse if you open the

windows and you can use yellow sticky traps to attract the adults. Allow the orchid to dry out between waterings to minimise any remote chance of the flies laying eggs in the medium. Fungus gnat eggs and larvae require moist soil and soon die if they dry out.

Why are there white marks and red, white or black spots on my orchid's leaves?

If this happens in spring or summer, and it is accompanied by the leaves turning yellowish or pale green, it is very likely to be damage from direct sunlight. Move the orchid to a shadier position and the plant should recover in time. The spots will not heal, and it is likely that the leaf around the white spots will turn black due to bacterial infection. Unless the plant has plenty of leaves, it is best not to cut the affected leaves off before the plant makes some new ones. Make sure you feed the plant regularly to aid recovery.

Direct sunlight damage on pseudobulbs of a Cambria-type orchid (Brassia) *(above),* Cattleya *leaf (below left) and* Phalaenopsis *leaf (below).*

What is causing white 'threads' on the leaves, white fluffy insects in the plant crevices or a cotton wool-like mass on some soft parts of my orchid?

Your orchid is most likely infected with mealybugs, very common sap-feeding insects. Remove the threads and any insects with a cotton bud dipped in alcohol and wipe the leaves clean regularly to prevent an infestation. See page 50 for more information on prevention and treatment.

Mealybugs hiding between the leaves and cane of Dendrobium nobile.

Signs of mealybug infestation on the underside of a Phalaenopsis *leaf.*

Why are the leaves on my orchid twisted? -or- Why have some leaves got split ends?

This is due to low humidity and often occurs with *Phalaenopsis* when they are kept near a radiator. Spray the orchid regularly and make sure it does not dry out as much between waterings, or move the orchid to a more humid position. You could also sit the orchid on a humidity tray (see page 20).

Phalaenopsis *leaves with split ends.*

Why are the leaves sticky, particularly underneath the tip? -or- What are the sticky droplets on the stem of my orchid?

This may be a natural extract made by the plant, or it could be a secretion left by insects, either scale insects, mealybugs or tiny red spider mites (see pages 50–52).

Look carefully for any insects; it is not always easy to see them. If there are any remove them by wiping the leaves with cotton wool dipped in alcohol. Wiping off the sticky substance will prevent sooty mould. If the problem persists, spray with a systemic or contact insecticide.

If there are no insects on the orchid, the sticky droplets are probably a natural excretion produced by the plant called 'guttation', which is either as a response to stress (usually too much water) or in order to attract insects such as ants. In the wild, ants are welcome as they protect the plants from other plant-eating insects, like beetles and thrips, but in the home environment they can spread diseases from one plant to another. Whatever the cause, it is best to remove any residue with a wet cloth. There is no need to spray with an insecticide.

*Guttation on a Cambria-type (*Brassia*) orchid.*

SIGNS

Damaged leaves with black, white or brown marks on a *Phalaenopsis*.

DIAGNOSIS

This is direct sunlight damage. The damaged part reflects the area where the sunlight directly hits the leaf through the glass. It is very likely that the orchid was moved recently to direct sunlight as the rest of the leaf is green.

TREATMENT

The plant has enough leaves, so cut both affected leaves back to healthy tissue and move the plant away from direct sunlight.

SIGNS

This *Phalaenopsis* has few leaves and no sign of healthy roots in the pot. The bark in the pot is black.

DIAGNOSIS

There are few healthy roots and the bark is broken down, both symptoms of too frequent watering.

TREATMENT

Remove the plant from the pot and inspect the roots. If there are a few roots, repot the plant in fresh bark. If there are no roots either discard the plant or put it in a polythene bag to keep high humidity around the plant until you see signs of new roots.

SIGNS

A poorly-looking Cambria-type orchid with yellow leaves and shrivelled pseudobulbs.

DIAGNOSIS

The likely cause is a poor root system, which makes it difficult for the plant to take up water. It looks like the roots have been damaged by too frequent watering.

TREATMENT

Remove the plant from the pot and check its root system. If roots are severely damaged or dead, remove dead roots and repot in fresh bark. Place in a bright, cool room. Water carefully until you see signs of new roots and growth.

SIGNS

◀ This *Phalaenopsis* has floppy leaves and few visible roots. The plant is unstable in its pot.

DIAGNOSIS

The leaves are dehydrated as the orchid has not been watered correctly. The plant was not repotted correctly and there is not enough bark in the pot.

TREATMENT

Soak the whole plant in tepid water for 20–30 minutes and repeat after a week if the leaves have not gained any vigour. Cut off the flower stem down to base so the plant can focus its energy on recovery. Repot after a week when roots are fully hydrated into the same size pot (see page 30).

SIGNS

This orchid is sitting proud of its pot with few aerial roots. The roots inside the pot do not look very healthy.

DIAGNOSIS

This *Phalaenopsis* needs repotting.

TREATMENT

Repot the plant following the instructions on page 30. Remove the bottom pair of leaves.

SIGNS

◀ Yellow bottom leaves, top roots look hard, yellow mark on the leaf.

DIAGNOSIS

This *Phalaenopsis* is in relatively good health but the yellow leaves are due to incorrect watering and insufficient nutrition. The top of the roots are dark due to exposure. The yellow mark is insect damage but not serious.

TREATMENT

The orchid is due to be repotted. You can remove the bottom two leaves. Use a 'Bloom' type fertiliser with every other watering to improve the general health of the plant.

SIGNS

All flowers (or buds) dried at the same time, possibly a dry leaf or two.

DIAGNOSIS

This *Dendrobium phalaenopsis* got too dry. The flowers (or buds), being the most sensitive part of the plant, suffered first.

TREATMENT

The plant should recover after a good watering. Adjust future waterings so it does not get too dry.

Before treatment

After treatment

SIGNS

◀ A poorly-looking old *Phalaenopsis* with few leaves, a couple with black spots, and a very large stem ('neck').

DIAGNOSIS

This plant is long overdue repotting. It has a good number of aerial roots (spray these daily for a week before repotting). The leaves are damaged due to direct sunlight and subsequent bacterial infection. The stem needs to be cut down to about 5 cm (2 in).

TREATMENT

Repot the orchid into an appropriately sized pot (see page 31).

SIGNS

This *Phalaenopsis* has twisted leaves and shrivelled roots.

DIAGNOSIS

The plant has suffered from low humidity and incorrect (insufficient) watering.

TREATMENT

Water the plant immediately and increase the frequency of future waterings to avoid drying out. Spray the plant regularly and/or place it on a humidity tray to avoid further twisting of the leaves.

SIGNS

Damaged leaves with white, brown or black marks.

DIAGNOSIS

Direct sunlight damage on a *Phalaenopsis*.

TREATMENT

Cut the severely damaged leaf back to healthy tissue but keep the other one (on the left) as this plant does not have many leaves. Move the plant away from direct sunlight.

SIGNS

The orchid is leaning towards one side. Few roots outside the pots and increasingly large leaves.

DIAGNOSIS

It is likely this *Phalaenopsis* has grown in a position of low light, with significantly more light on one side. Split and twisted leaves indicate that the plant is growing in a low-humidity environment.

TREATMENT

Repot, retaining all roots, into a slightly larger pot (12 to 13 cm). Remove the bottom leaves so the orchid can be placed at the right level for the newly emerging roots to go into the bark. Spray the plant regularly or place it on a humidity tray. The new flower spike is visible and the plant should be flowering soon.

Before treatment

SIGNS

A *Phalaenopsis* with few leaves, some red, some twisted. The root tips are black.

DIAGNOSIS

The orchid is due for repotting. The twisted leaves are due to low humidity and the red leaves are due to bright light. The damaged roots at the bottom are because the orchid was allowed to sit in water. The plant is due for repotting.

TREATMENT

Repot into fresh bark and remove the bottom leaf. Use a urea-free fertiliser with every other watering.

After treatment

SIGNS

A new leaf that has turned yellow and later brown (as opposed to old leaves turning yellow which can be old age or incorrect watering).

DIAGNOSIS

The most likely cause for this on a Cambria orchid is a very wet substrate. It often happens when cambrias are grown in coir especially during winter when the plant does not need as much watering.

TREATMENT

Adjust watering so the medium is not overly wet, and if possible, repot the orchid in bark next spring (see page 34).

SIGNS

The tissue is brown at the end or side of a Cambria leaf.

DIAGNOSIS

This is tissue damage due to cold. The most likely cause is that the leaf has been touching a very cold window. The light brown tissue is earlier damage which has dried; the darker brown is more recent damage.

TREATMENT

Cut the leaf back to healthy tissue and make sure the leaves of the plant don't touch the cold window. Ideally move the plant from that position as it seems to be too cold for it.

15 months later

SIGNS

This *Dendrobium nobile* has many roots outside the pot and the pot is full of roots. Several of the pseudobulbs are not staked.

DIAGNOSIS

The orchid is overdue for repotting.

TREATMENT

As the orchid has just finished flowering, this is a good time to repot. Use a slightly larger pot (11 cm or 13 cm), stake the pseudobulbs and remove any yellow leaves.

SIGNS

Sudden loss of flowers. The plant has few leaves, dry aerial roots and few roots inside the pot.

DIAGNOSIS

This orchid has been watered incorrectly and kept dry for long periods. The plant is relatively healthy but it has been given the minimum water it requires for survival.

TREATMENT

This *Phalaenopsis* will benefit from repotting in the same size pot and more frequent watering, as well as regular spraying to bring the roots back to good health. Cut the flower stem back to base.

Before treatment

SIGNS

Few hard leaves and many aerial roots. Black roots outside and inside the pot, and the orchid has a long stem ('neck').

DIAGNOSIS

This *Phalaenopsis* has been allowed to sit in water, which killed all the roots in the pot. The leaves and aerial roots are hard, due to high light and lack of spraying. It should have been repotted a long time ago.

TREATMENT

Repot into fresh bark after removing the bottom part of the stem and all the damaged leaves and dead roots.

After treatment

SIGNS

A Cambria-type orchid with too many aerial roots.

DIAGNOSIS

The plant and the aerial roots are in good health due to regular spraying. The orchid is due for repotting.

TREATMENT

Repot and possibly divide the orchid into two (see page 34).

SIGNS

The orchid has not grown any new leaves for some time; the roots look healthy but the leaves are turning yellow and the middle of the orchid looks very brown.

DIAGNOSIS

The centre or core of this *Phalaenopsis* rotted some time ago. The most likely cause is damp and cold conditions, which can occur in conservatories or damp corners of the house (not as likely to occur in a centrally heated house).

TREATMENT

Sadly the situation is terminal. If the orchid loses its main meristem, its principal growing point, it is destined to die. Sometimes a 'strong' orchid will grow a new shoot on its side which may flower after few years. On this occasion this has not happened, and the orchid is best disposed of.

SIGNS

◀ Hard, smallish, reddish leaves on a **Phalaenopsis** orchid.

DIAGNOSIS

Too much light (probably accompanied by high temperatures) but not direct enough to cause damage to the leaf. This orchid is likely to have been growing in a south-facing, semi-shaded conservatory.

TREATMENT

Move the plant to a position where it receives less light to improve its long-term health.

Before treatment

SIGNS

Yellow leaves, overgrown plant, brown markings on the side of the pot. ▶

DIAGNOSIS

The yellow leaves of this *Paphiopedilum* are due to age, direct light and incorrect feeding. The plant is due for repotting and possibly dividing. The brown markings on the side of the pot are salts which have accumulated because the orchid has been standing in water.

TREATMENT

Repot and possibly divide the plant, remove old leaves and don't allow standing in water.

After treatment

SIGNS

Sunken sections or small holes on the leaf (perhaps with black areas around them).

DIAGNOSIS

Insect damage, probably a few weeks ago. Any black areas around the 'bites' are due to bacterial infection.

TREATMENT

Inspect the plant for insects and remove mechanically. If appropriate use a systemic or contact insectiside. If no insects are found (which is more likely) there is no need to do anything.

SIGNS

◀ This flowering *Phalaenopsis* has few leaves, and a few dry aerial roots outside the pot.

DIAGNOSIS

The orchid is growing in a high light environment and/or has been flowering profusely without time to make leaves in between flowerings. The aerial roots in combination with the good root system inside the pot indicate that it needs repotting.

TREATMENT

Feed with a 'Grow' formulation, and spray regularly to make the roots malleable. The plant needs repotting when it finishes flowering.

Before treatment

SIGNS

This Cambria orchid (*Oncidium*) is leaning to one side and the new roots that will grow from the newer pseudobulbs will be hanging in the air outside the pot.

DIAGNOSIS

The orchid needs repotting after flowering is finished.

TREATMENT

The orchid has been repotted in a clear pot with room to grow for another two years. A year later it is doing well, and is in flower with two spikes.

One year after treatment

After extensive research we strongly recommend the following products. In our experience, they give consistently superb results.

Orchid Myst
(by Growth Technology Ltd)

A simple and convenient way to feed orchids and provide them with nutrients. It is the best orchid foliar feed on the market as it contains humic acid, which is a great organic enhancer that makes nutrients more easily available to the plant.

Orchid Focus Repotting Mix
(by Growth Technology Ltd)

Superb quality, graded bark. Peat free, as orchid media should be. The only widely available orchid growing medium we would use for our orchids.

Orchid Focus Bloom
Orchid Focus Grow
(by Growth Technology Ltd)

Specifically formulated for orchids, they contain all the essential nutrients, as well as humic acid. Urea free, as orchid fertilisers should be, and great value for money. By far the best fertilisers on the market.

Orchid Ultra
(by Growth Technology Ltd)

This is a good growth enhancer specifically for orchids – not a fertiliser. It is not necessary normally, but good to use when the plant is under stress or you want to help it make more roots.

SB Plant Invigorator
(by Stan Brouard Ltd)

A great contact insecticide for use with orchids. It will control most common orchid pests including mealybugs, spider mites, whitefly and aphids.

Orchiata Bark
(by Besgrow BV)

Excellent quality bark and a good alternative for species that do not need regular repotting.

Botani-Wipe

The natural plant and leaf polish wipe. Biodegradable, non-toxic. Contains 100% pure neem oil.

Orchid-Pro™
(by Dyna-Gro)

Orchid-Pro™ 7-8-6 is a well-balanced, professional formulation containing all essential macro- and micronutrients for use on all types of orchids. It provides the right balance of nutrients for healthy growth and flowering. Urea free.

Orchids pots
(various manufacturers)

All these pots are ideal for all orchids as they have an air cone and good drainage.

Most *Cymbidium* orchids are best repotted in tall pots with very good drainage.

**This book is dedicated to
Manos's mum, Georgia, and Peter's sister, Janice**

We have worked hard at trying to provide all the necessary information about growing orchids at home in an easy-to-understand way. If you have any feedback about the book, or a particular problem with your orchids, feel free to contact us at manoseag@gmail.com.

Acknowledgements

Many thanks to Sam Stanley for her help with editing, as well as Louise, Jenny, Marta, Monica, Eleni, Kim, Clair and Sarah for lending us their orchids and general help. Also thanks to Kew botanical horticulturalist, Bala Kompalli, Kew botanist Andre Schuiteman, as well as to Lydia White and Gina Fullerlove from Kew Publishing and to Michelle Payne for proofreading the book.
Special thanks to Steve Balcombe for the photography, design and page layout.

Photo credits

Royal Botanic Gardens, Kew: front cover image.
Javadoplant: images on pages 13, 14 (good plant to buy), page 29 (all), page 44 (hanging *Vanda*).
AirPixa Ltd: page 68 (the divided *Paphiopedilum*)
Manos Kanellos: page 9
Steve Balcombe: images on page 4 (orchid flower), 12, 14 (top flower), 17–22, 25–27, 28 (top and left), 30–31, 32 (bottom orchid), 34, 38, 39, 41, 42, 44 (centre and right), 47 (bottom image), 48 (bottom image), 49–51, 54–57, 58 (keiki images), 59–70, 71 (wipes, SB Plant Invigorator, and pots), back cover (picture of M. Kanellos).
Shutterstock: images on inside front cover; pages 3, 4 (*Cymbidium*), 5–8, 10, 15, 23–24, 28 (blue orchid), 32 (top image), 33, 35–37, 40, 43, 45–46, 47 (top image), 48 (top image), 51–52, 58 (bottom image); inside back cover; back cover (orchid images).